Take-Home Leveled Readers

On-level

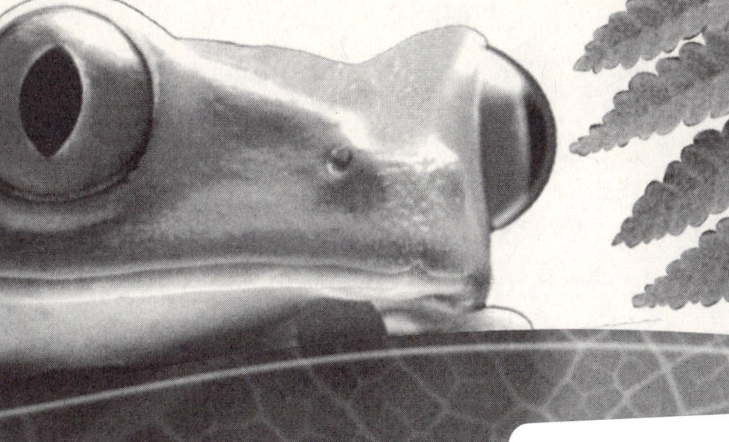

Science

Editorial Offices: Glenview, Illinois • Parsippany, New Jersey • New York, New York
Sales Ofices: Needham, Massachusetts • Duluth, Georgia • Glenview, Illinois
Coppell, Texas • Sacramento, California • Mesa, Arizona

PEARSON
Scott
Foresman

sfsuccessnet.com

ISBN: 0-328-19722-X

2 3 4 5 6 7 8 9 10 V004 13 12 11 10 09 08 07 06 05

Table of Contents

To the Teacher

Scott Foresman provides three Leveled Readers for every chapter of *Scott Foresman Science*, Grades 1–6: a *Below-Level Leveled Reader*, an *On-Level Leveled Reader*, and an *Advanced Leveled Reader*.

All three readers teach the same science concepts, same vocabulary, address the same target reading skill and contain the same graphic organizer as the corresponding student edition chapter, just at three different reading levels—providing access to important science content for all students. The On-level and Advanced readers also use additional examples to enrich the chapter and extend ideas

This book contains reproducible copies of the On-Level Leveled Readers for Grade 2. These are designed for you to reproduce and send home with your students as appropriate. Encourage students to share these books with parents or family members in order to practice reading skills and reinforce science content.

Online versions of these and other readers are also available through the Scott Foresman Leveled Reader Database.

Plants

by Christine Wolf

Science

Genre	Comprehension Skill	Text Features	Science Content
Nonfiction	Predict	• Captions • Call Outs • Labels • Glossary	Plants

Scott Foresman Science 2.1

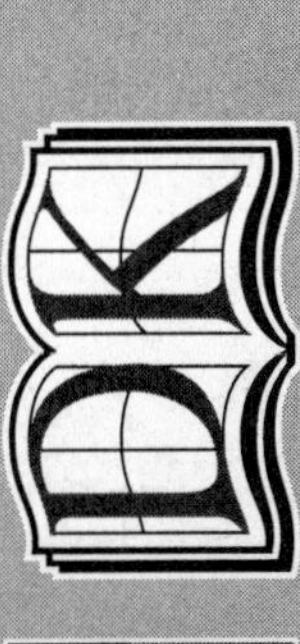

PEARSON

Scott Foresman

scottforesman.com

ISBN 0-328-13770-7

1

What did you learn?

1. What are the four main parts of a plant?

2. What is a prairie?

3. **Writing** in Science Desert plants are adapted to live where it is hot and dry. Their spines help them live in this environment. In your own words write to explain how spines can help a cactus plant survive in the desert.

4. **Predict** Sundew plants live in marshes. They have sticky hairs on their leaves. Predict what will happen to an insect that lands on a sundew plant.

Vocabulary

adapted
environment
flower
leaves
nutrients
prairie
roots
stem

Picture Credits
Every effort has been made to secure permission and provide appropriate credit for photographic material.
The publisher deeply regrets any omission and pledges to correct errors called to its attention in subsequent editions.

Photo locators denoted as follows: Top (T), Center (C), Bottom (B), Left (L), Right (R), Background (Bkgd).

Opener: Gerry Ellis/Digital Vision; 14 (B) Jacqui Hurst/DK Images; 15 (BL) Eric Crichton/Corbis; 21 Kevin Schafer/Corbis.

Unless otherwise acknowledged, all photographs are the copyright © of Dorling Kindersley, a division of Pearson.

ISBN: 0-328-13770-7

Glossary

adapted	changed in order to live in a certain environment
environment	all the living and nonliving things surrounding a plant or an animal
flower	the part of a plant that makes seeds
leaves	the food-making part of a plant
nutrients	materials that living things need to live and grow
prairie	a place with lots of grass and few trees
roots	the parts of a plant that take in water and nutrients from the soil
stem	the part of a plant that carries water and nutrients to the leaves

Plants

by Christine Wolf

Parts of a Plant

There are many kinds of plants. Plants are made up of different parts. Each part has a job. The parts help the plant get the things it needs to live.

Nutrients are materials that living things need to live and grow. They are found in soil and water.

What does a plant need to live?

- water
- air
- sunlight
- space
- nutrients

cactus

cattail

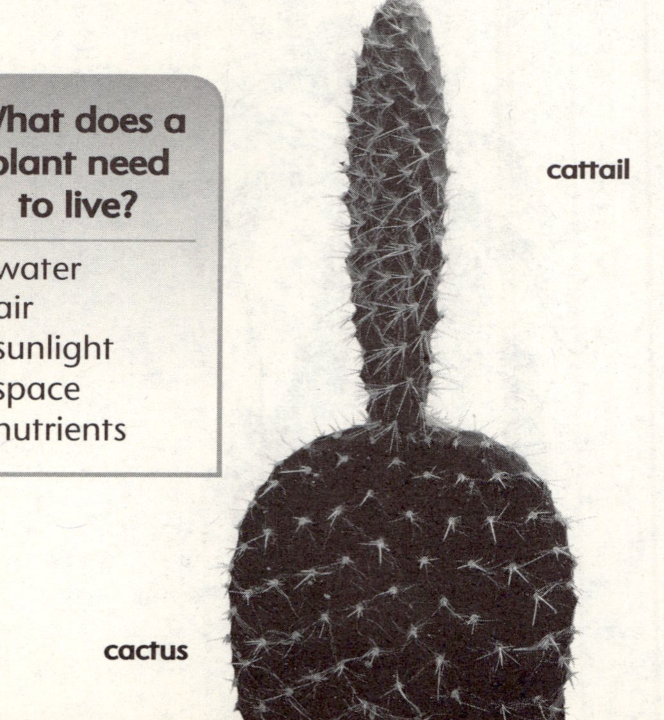

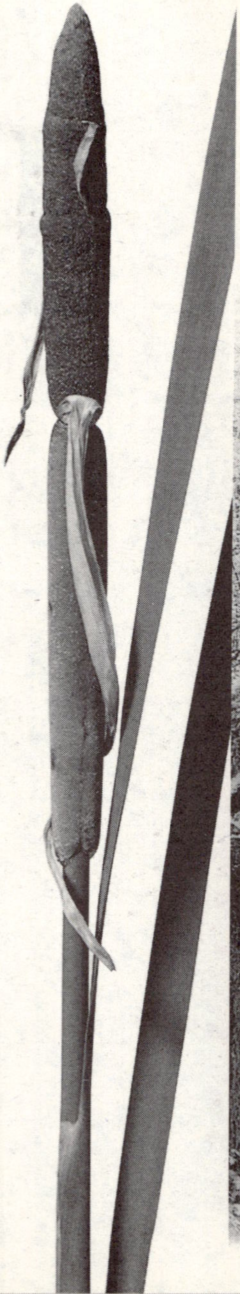

Plants come in all shapes and sizes. They can live almost anywhere. What kind of plants live where you live?

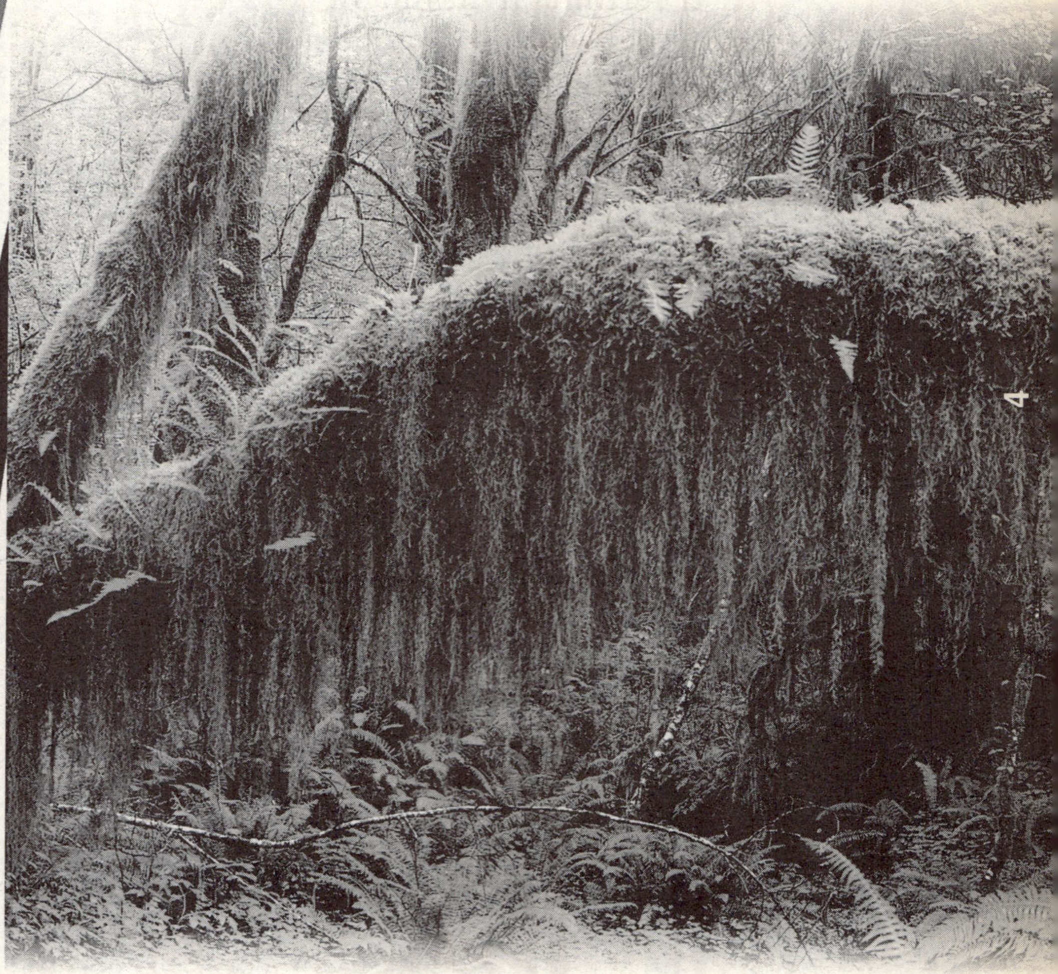

Plants in Marsh Environments

A marsh is a very wet environment. Its soil does not have many nutrients. Plants in a marsh environment are adapted to live in this kind of soil.

Pitcher plants trap insects to get nutrients! Insects like to crawl into the plant. Then the plant snaps shut.

flowering plant

Plants have four main parts. The parts are roots, stem, leaves, and flowers.

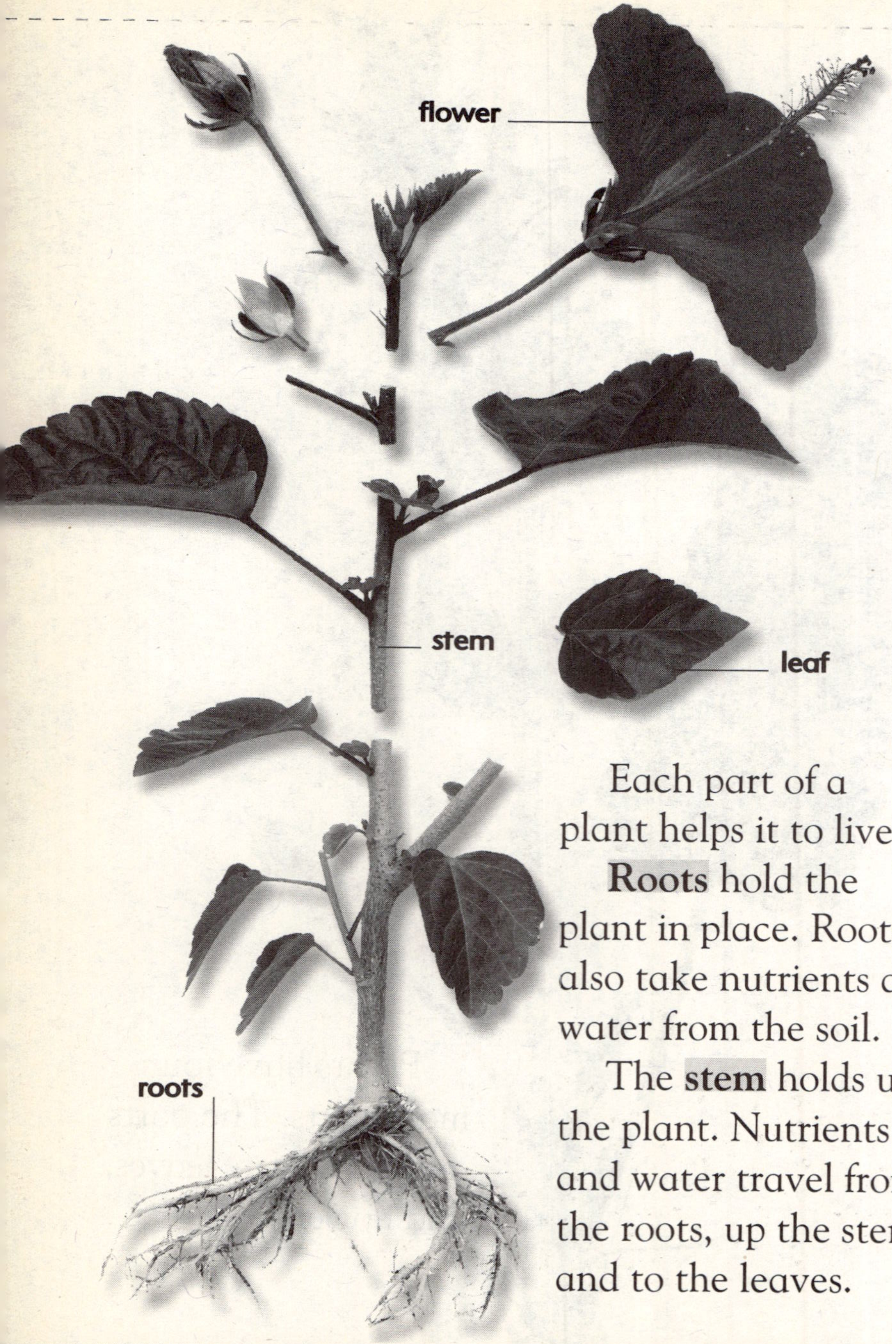

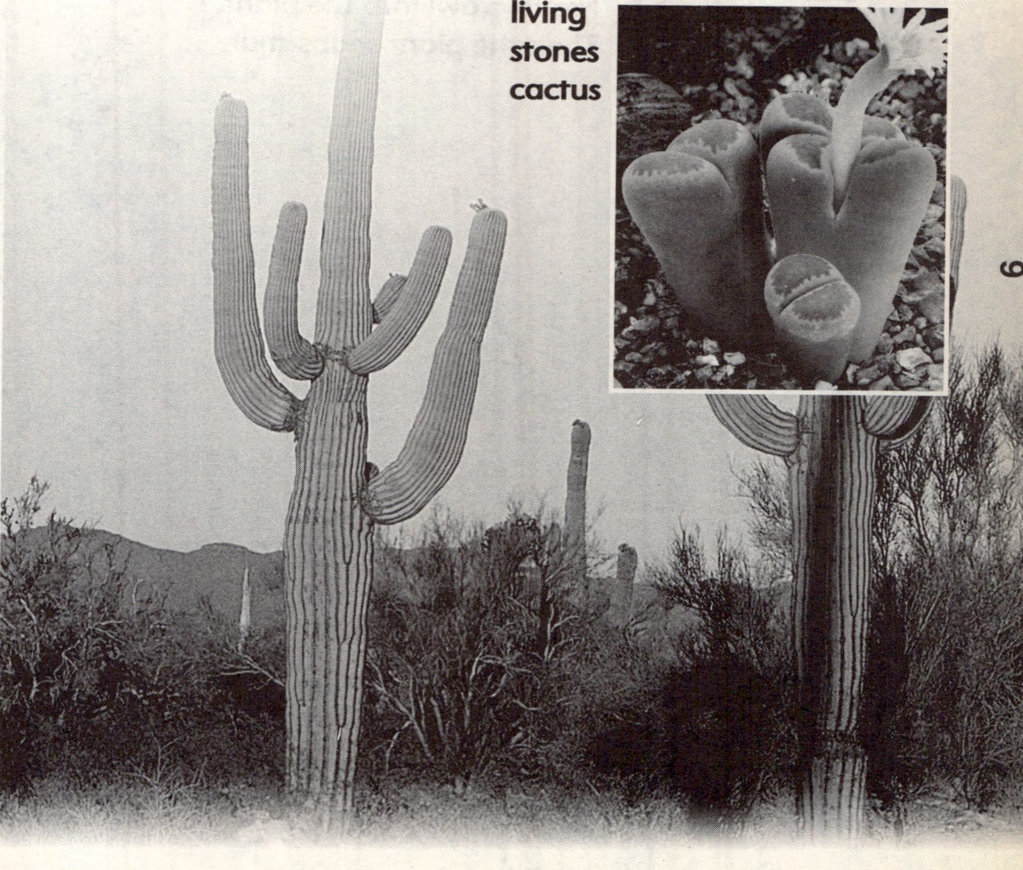

Each part of a plant helps it to live.

Roots hold the plant in place. Roots also take nutrients and water from the soil.

The **stem** holds up the plant. Nutrients and water travel from the roots, up the stem, and to the leaves.

The spine tips of a cactus also hold dewdrops. The dew drips into the soil and feeds the plant.

The cactus plants called living stones are adapted to look like real stones. That way, thirsty desert animals will not eat them!

living stones cactus

Plants in Desert Environments

A desert environment can be very hot in the day and cold at night. There is very little rain in the desert.

The barrel cactus is adapted to the desert's dry heat. It stores water inside. Its sharp spines protect the cactus from thirsty animals.

The stem of this young tree is short. The stem of this tree is very tall.

Leaves are a plant's food factory. Leaves use sunlight, air, and water to make food for a plant.

Plants in Prairie Environments

A **prairie** is an environment with lots of grass and few trees.

Summers there can be very hot. Little rain falls in the prairie. Some prairie plants are adapted to hold water.

The flowering spurge is adapted to life in a prairie. It has very deep roots. The roots find water even when there is little rain.

Plants Living Near Water

Some plants live on or near water. They are adapted to living in a wet environment.

Water lilies are adapted to live in ponds. Their leaves are wide and green. They can float on the water and catch the sunlight. This way, they can get what they need to make food for the plant.

Many plants have flowers. A **flower** makes seeds. Seeds grow into new plants.

Scattering Seeds

Seeds need space to grow. To *scatter* means to "spread out." When seeds are scattered, they find space to grow.

Seeds can be scattered by people. They can be scattered by water. Seeds can be scattered by air or wind. Animals scatter seeds too.

These dandelion seeds will be scattered by air.

Scotch pine trees have waxy needles for leaves. These thin needles are not hurt by ice or frost. Sweet gum trees are also adapted to the seasons. The large, shiny leaves are green in spring and summer. The leaves change color and fall off when it gets cold. This helps the tree store food and water for the winter.

sweet gum tree

Plants in Woodland Environments

In a woodland environment there are seasons. The plants there live through cold winters, warm and wet springs, hot summers, and cool falls.

Plants in woodland environments are adapted to live in these changing seasons.

needles of scotch pine

Coconuts are seeds. They scatter by floating on water.

Flowering And Nonflowering Plants

Plants fit into two groups. One group of plants grows flowers. The other group does not grow flowers.

Plants with flowers come in all shapes and sizes. A daisy is a plant that grows flowers.

Plants are **adapted** to live in different environments. This means they have special parts that help them live in all kinds of places.

Where Plants Grow

Plants grow in many different places. Living and nonliving things around a plant are called that plant's **environment.**

This orange tree also grows flowers. The flowers make fruits that cover and protect the seeds.

Plants Without Flowers

Some plants do not have flowers.
They still have ways to make new plants.
Pine trees do not have flowers. They
have cones. Seeds fall out of the cones.
New trees grow from the seeds.

pinecone

Mosses and ferns can grow in wet,
shady places. They do not have flowers.
They do not even have seeds! These
plants have other parts to help them
make new plants.

Animal Groups

by Carol Levine

Genre	Comprehension Skill	Text Features	Science Content
Nonfiction	Alike and Different	• Call Outs • Glossary	Vertebrates and Invertebrates

Scott Foresman Science 2.2

PEARSON

Scott Foresman

scottforesman.com

ISBN 0-328-13773-1

What did you learn?

1. How does an arctic fox's fur change in the winter?

2. How does camouflage protect a chameleon?

3. **Writing** in Science Snails and jellyfish do not have backbones. Write to explain how these animals stay safe. Include details from the book to support your answer.

4. **Alike and Different** How is an octopus like an earthworm? How is it different?

Vocabulary

amphibian
bird
camouflage
fish
gills
insect
mammal
reptile

Picture Credits
Every effort has been made to secure permission and provide appropriate credit for photographic material.
The publisher deeply regrets any omission and pledges to correct errors called to its attention in subsequent editions.

Photo locators denoted as follows: Top (T), Center (C), Bottom (B), Left (L), Right (R), Background (Bkgd).

Minden Pictures: 1 (TL): © Natural History Museum, London/DK Images; 4 (BC) © Jerry Young/DK Images;
5 (CR): © Pete Atkinson/NHPA; 6–7: © Norbert Rosing/National Geographic Image Collection;
7 (C): © Jerry Young/DK Images; 10–11: © Pete Atkinson/NHPA; 11 (C): © Norbert Wu/Minden Pictures;
16–17: © David Wrobel/Visuals Unlimited; 18: © Natural History Museum, London/DK Images;
19: © Natural History Museum, London/DK Images; 22: © Jeff Rotman/Nature Picture Library.

Unless otherwise acknowledged, all photographs are the copyright © of Dorling Kindersley, a division of Pearson.

ISBN: 0-328-13773-1

Glossary

amphibian	an animal with a backbone and smooth, wet skin that lives on land and in water
bird	an animal with a backbone, feathers, and wings that hatches from an egg
camouflage	a color or shape that makes an animal hard to see
fish	an animal with a backbone, scales, and fins that lives in water
gills	body parts that help fish get oxygen from water
insect	an animal with three body parts and six legs that does not have a backbone
mammal	an animal with a backbone and hair or fur
reptile	an animal with a backbone and scales that hatches from an egg

Animal
Groups

by Carol Levine

2

Introduction

There are many kinds of animals. Animals belong to different groups. Different animals have different body parts. The parts an animal has can tell us which group it is in.

Animals with backbones live in many places in the world. Animals without backbones do too. Wherever an animal lives, it is adapted to its environment.

Octopuses

Octopuses are sea animals without backbones. They can make clouds of ink to stay safe. Ink makes it hard for other animals to find octopuses. Octopuses can also use camouflage to hide.

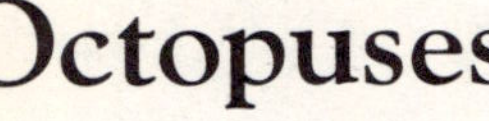

One group of animals has backbones. Bones help animals move. Bones give animals their shape. Bones can even protect an animal's other body parts.

Animals with Backbones

There are many groups of animals with backbones. **Mammals, birds, fish, reptiles,** and **amphibians** are all groups of animals with backbones.

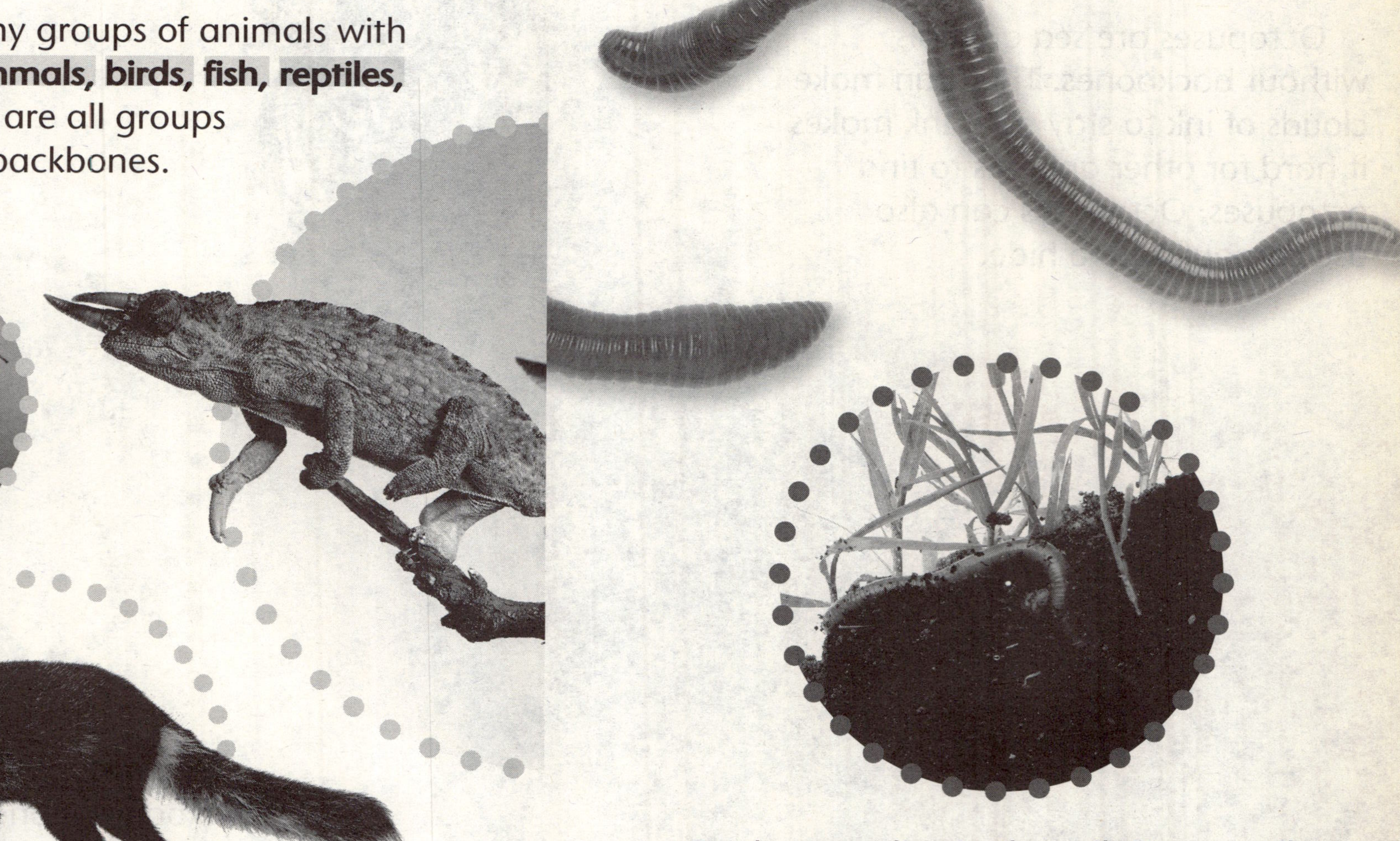

Earthworms live in the soil. Damp soil helps keep the skin of the worms wet. They must stay damp to be able to get air.

Worms

There are lots of different kinds of worms. Worms do not have backbones. Earthworms' bodies have more than one hundred parts.

Even though these animals have backbones, they are different from one another. Animals are different because they live in different environments. Animals have adapted to their environment.

Mammals

Some animals are mammals. Mammals have backbones. Most mammals have fur or hair on their bodies. Mammals live in many different environments. Mammals are adapted to live in their environment.

Like all insects, the cicada (suh KAY duh) does not have bones. The cicada can sing. The loud singing of some cicadas keeps them safe. Birds do not like this sound. They stay away from the cicadas.

Insects

Insects have three main body parts and six legs. Many insects have antennae on their heads. These antennae help the insects feel, smell, hear, and taste things.

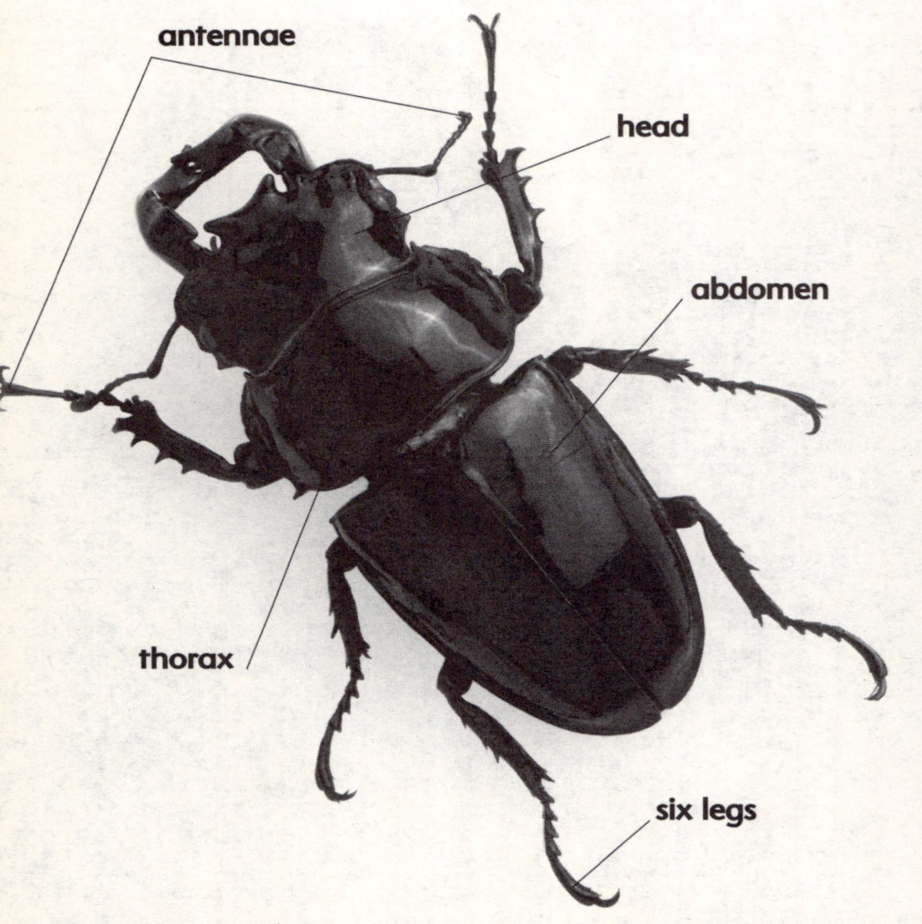

Some mammals change colors to hide in their environment. This is called **camouflage.** One mammal that uses camouflage is the arctic fox. In winter the fox's fur changes from gray or brown to white. This helps the fox hide in the snow.

Animals without backbones need to protect their body parts too. Snails have soft bodies. Their hard shells help them stay safe. Jellyfish also have soft bodies. But they can sting animals that want to harm them.

Birds

Some animals are birds. Birds have backbones. They have feathers and wings. Many birds use their feathers and wings to fly.

Birds also live in many different environments. Birds are adapted to live in their environment.

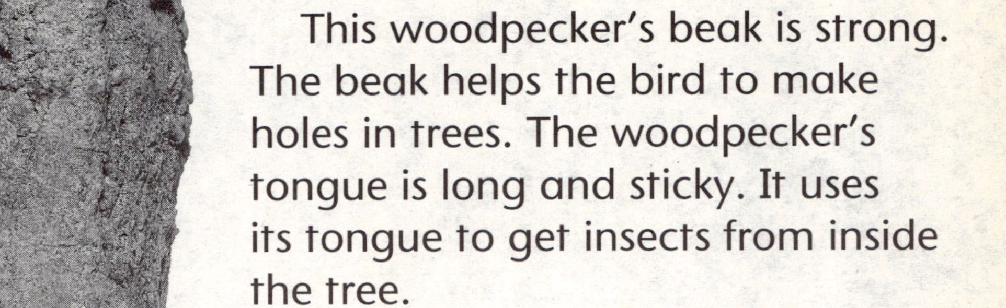

Animals Without Backbones

There are many animals in the world that do not have backbones. Animals without backbones live in many different environments. They are adapted to their environment.

This woodpecker's beak is strong. The beak helps the bird to make holes in trees. The woodpecker's tongue is long and sticky. It uses its tongue to get insects from inside the tree.

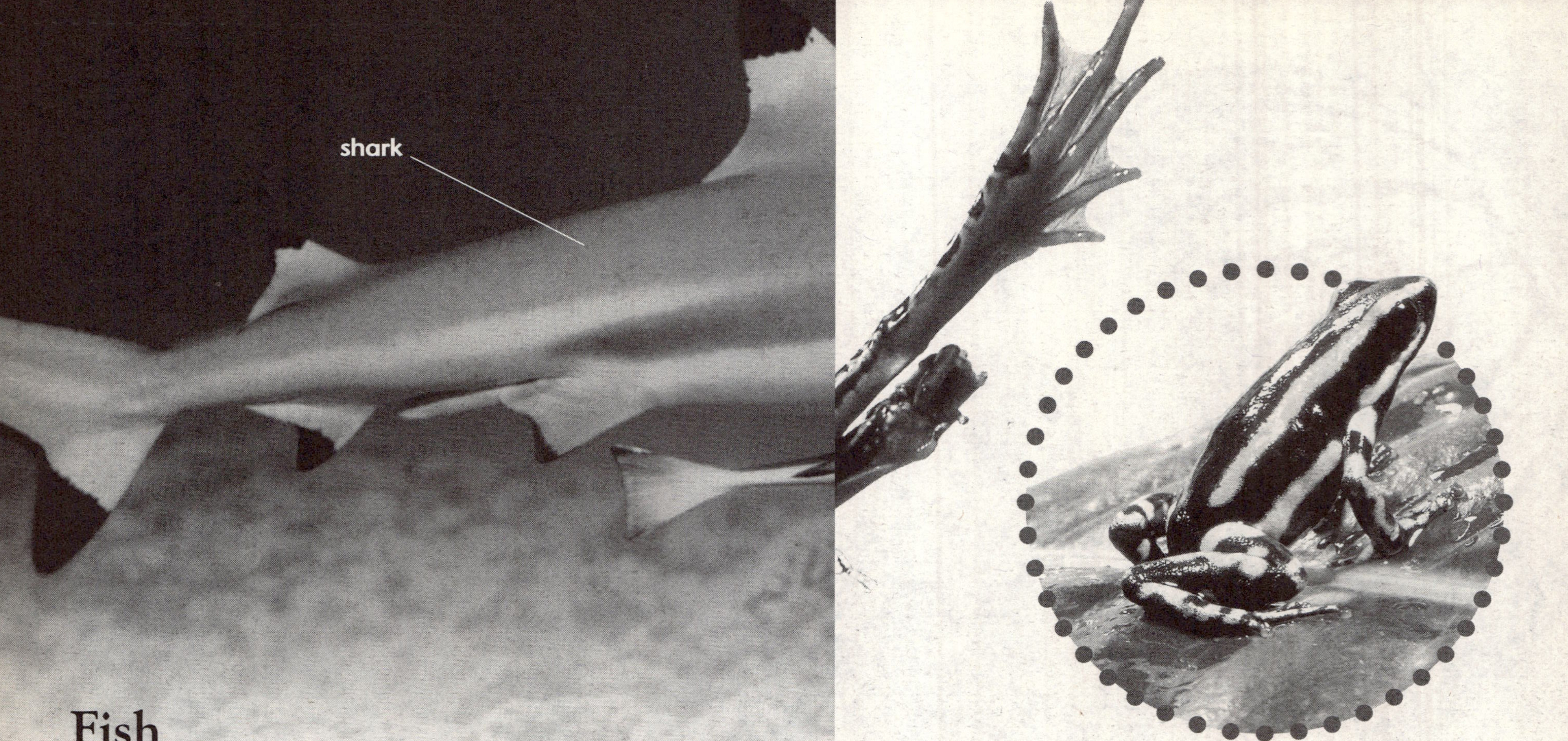

Fish

Some animals are fish. Some fish have backbones. Fish live in the water. Fish are adapted to live in this environment.

Most fish have scales. Most fish have fins. Scales and fins help fish swim. Fish have **gills.** Gills help fish get the oxygen they need to live.

This poison dart frog eats insects and turns them into poison. The poison travels through the frog's body and onto its skin. The poison keeps other animals from eating the frog. This way, the frog stays safe.

26

Amphibians

Some animals are amphibians. Amphibians have backbones. Amphibians live in many different environments. They can live on land and in the water. They are adapted to live in their environment.

The remora fish has a sucker on its head. This fish stays safe by using its sucker to stick to other sea animals. Sometimes remoras stick to sharks. Sharks keep remoras safe.

The chameleon can change from yellow to green to brown. Different things cause its skin color to change. Sometimes the color changes because the animal is afraid. Camouflage helps the chameleon stay safe.

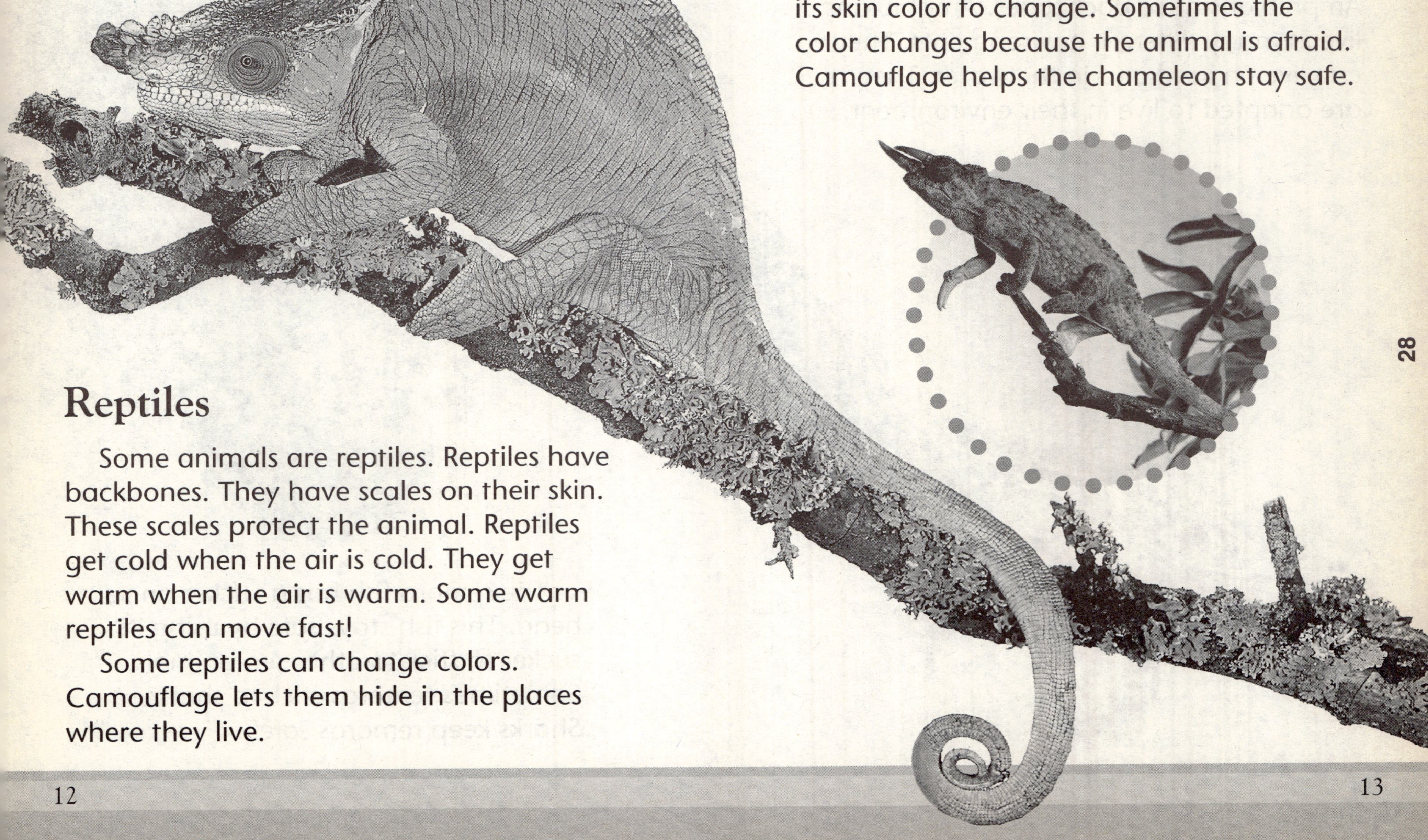

Reptiles

Some animals are reptiles. Reptiles have backbones. They have scales on their skin. These scales protect the animal. Reptiles get cold when the air is cold. They get warm when the air is warm. Some warm reptiles can move fast!

Some reptiles can change colors. Camouflage lets them hide in the places where they live.

Plants AND Animals

29

Genre	Comprehension Skill	Text Features	Science Content
Nonfiction	Cause and Effect	• Captions • Diagram • Glossary	Plants and Animals

Scott Foresman Science 2.3

PEARSON
Scott Foresman

DK

ISBN 0-328-13776-6

9 780328 137763

90000

scottforesman.com

by Evan Allen

What did you learn?

1. What is the difference between a producer and a consumer?

2. What can animals use to build nests?

3. **Writing** in Science Energy moves through a food chain. Write to explain how it moves. Use words from the book as you write.

4. **Cause and Effect** What happens when habitats cannot meet the needs of the plants and animals that live there?

Picture Credits
Every effort has been made to secure permission and provide appropriate credit for photographic material. The publisher deeply regrets any omission and pledges to correct errors called to its attention in subsequent editions.

Photo locators denoted as follows: Top (T), Center (C), Bottom (B), Left (L), Right (R), Background (Bkgd).

2 Andrew Plumptre/Photolibrary/OSF Limited; 7 Tom Vezo/Peter Arnold, Inc.; 8 Ferrero-Labat /Peter Arnold, Inc.; 9 (CR) ©Rick and Nora Bowers/Visuals Unlimited; 13 (BL) ©Darren Bennett/Animals Animals/Earth Scenes; 14 (BL) Amos Nachoum/Corbis; 15 (TR) Amos Nachoum/Corbis, (CL) ©Oxford University Museum/DK Images; 16 Alexis Rosenfeld/Photo Researchers, Inc.; 17 (C) Alexis Rosenfeld/Photo Researchers, Inc.; 18 Mark Moffett/Minden Pictures; 19 (B) © Gilbert Twiest /Visuals Unlimited; 21 Heather Angel/Natural Visions; 22 ©Steve Hopkin/Ardea.

Scott Foresman/Dorling Kindersley would also like to thank: 15 (CLA) Stephen Oliver/DK Images.

Unless otherwise acknowledged, all photographs are the copyright © of Dorling Kindersley, a division of Pearson.

ISBN: 0-328-13776-6

Plants AND Animals

by Evan Allen

Glossary

consumer   a living thing that eats other living things

food chain   how living things get energy from food

food web   more than one food chain in one place

predator   an animal that hunts and eats other animals

prey   animals that are hunted for food

producer   a living thing that makes its own food

Plants and Animals Have Needs

Plants and animals are living things. All living things have needs. Needs can be different for different living things. Plants need light from the Sun. Animals need shelter. All living things share some needs.

Plants and animals live together. They share needs. Living things help each other in many ways.

Dairy ants and aphids live together and help each other. The ants keep predators away from the aphids. The aphids make honeydew. The honeydew is a sweet treat for the ants to eat.

Plants and animals both need air. They both need water. They both need space. All living things need food.

Some living things can make their own food.
They are called **producers.** Plants are producers.
They use light from the Sun to make food in their
leaves and stems. Green plants can make food.

Animals Need Each Other

Animals need each other in many ways.
Animals work together. They can protect each
other. They can feed each other. They can give
each other a place to live.

**The oxpecker eats ticks that live on the rhino's
back. This keeps the rhino clean. The rhino and
the oxpecker need each other.**

Building Nests

Animals can use parts of plants and other animals to build nests. They can use leaves. They can use feathers.

What parts of plants and animals do you see in this nest?

Some living things cannot make food inside their own bodies. They are called **consumers.**
Consumers look for food in their habitats. Animals are consumers.

Cows need grass to eat.

Different Needs

Different animals have different needs.
Big animals need more food, water, and space.
Small animals need less food, water, and space.

**Which of these animals
needs more space?**

Yucca moths help yucca plants. They take
pollen from plant to plant. This helps new
plants grow.

Yucca plants help yucca moths. The moths
lay their eggs in the plants. When they hatch,
the young moths find shelter
in the plant.

**Yucca plants and yucca
moths help each other.**

36

Plants and Animals Help Each Other

Plants and animals can help each other. These wasps are getting food from a fig.

Plants and animals share habitats. They help each other to get what they need.

Sometimes habitats do not have enough food. When this happens some animals might die.

A gilded flicker nests in a cactus.

Getting Food
In a Grassland

Food chains show how living things get food. All food chains start with the Sun. Plants use energy from the Sun to make food. Animals eat those plants. Other animals eat those animals. These are the steps of a food chain.

gazelles grazing in
a grassland habitat

People can change food webs. When people throw trash in the ocean they hurt ocean food webs. People can help too. It helps when people try to keep the ocean clean.

Food Webs
Can Change

Lots of things can change a food web. Some changes can be bad. They hurt the plants and animals in the food web.

Energy passes from the Sun to the black-footed ferret in this food chain. Animals in food chains can be predators or prey. **Predators** catch and eat other animals. The animals they eat are **prey.**

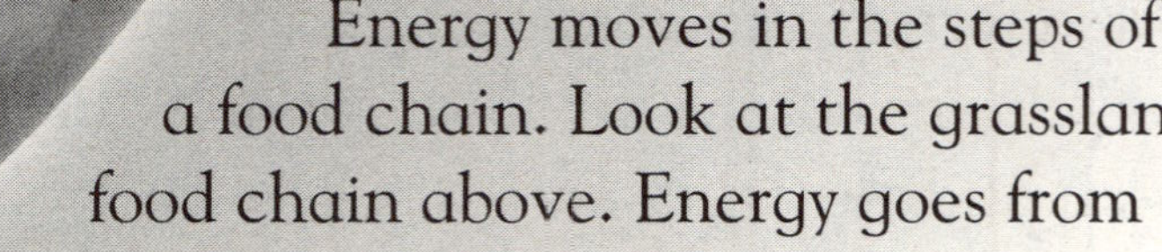

Energy moves in the steps of a food chain. Look at the grassland food chain above. Energy goes from the Sun to a daisy plant.

Ocean food chains make up food webs. Look at the plants and animals. How does energy move from the Sun to the orca?

Getting Food In an Ocean

An ocean is another habitat. Many plants and animals live there. These plants and animals get energy through food chains.

Look at the ocean food chain below. What animals are part of this food chain?

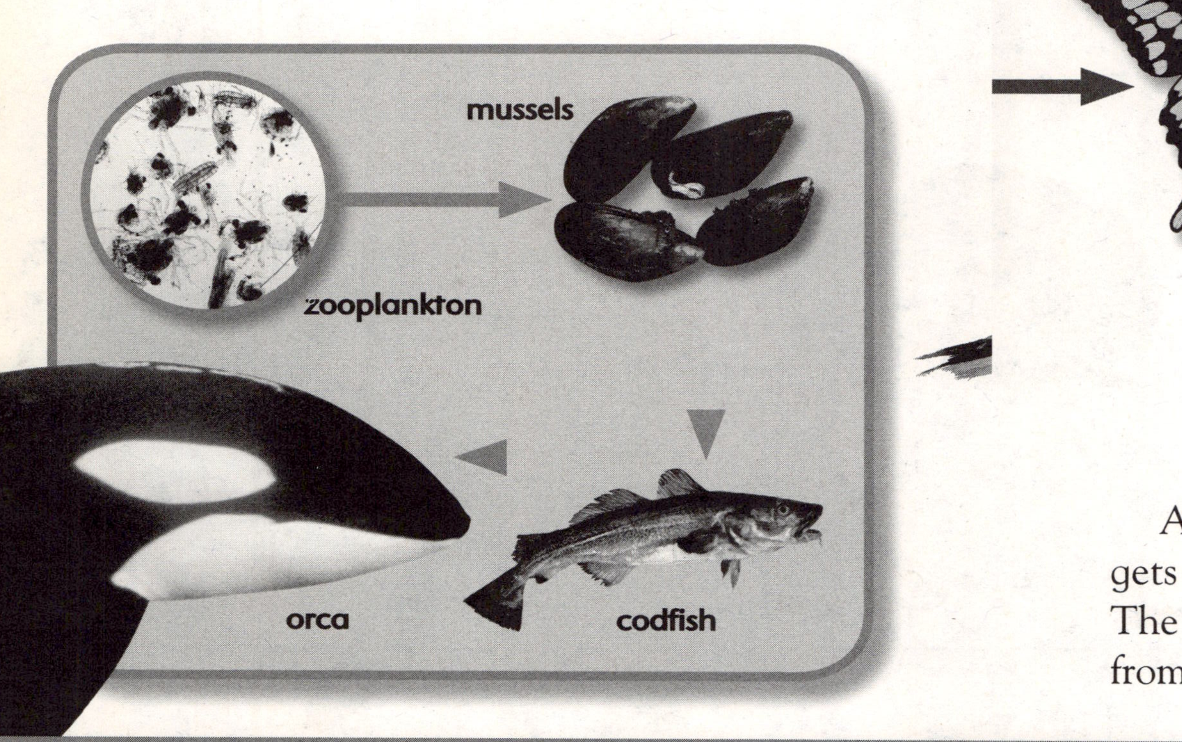

A butterfly feeds on the daisy. The butterfly gets energy too. A skink eats the butterfly. The skink gets energy. The energy has moved from the Sun to the skink.

Food Web in a Grassland

Habitats can have more than one food chain.
Grasslands have more than one food chain.
All the food chains in a grassland make up
a **food web.**

Look at the picture of a grassland food web.
The Sun helps plants make food. Some animals
eat the plants. Other animals eat those animals.
Follow the arrows to see the
different food chains.

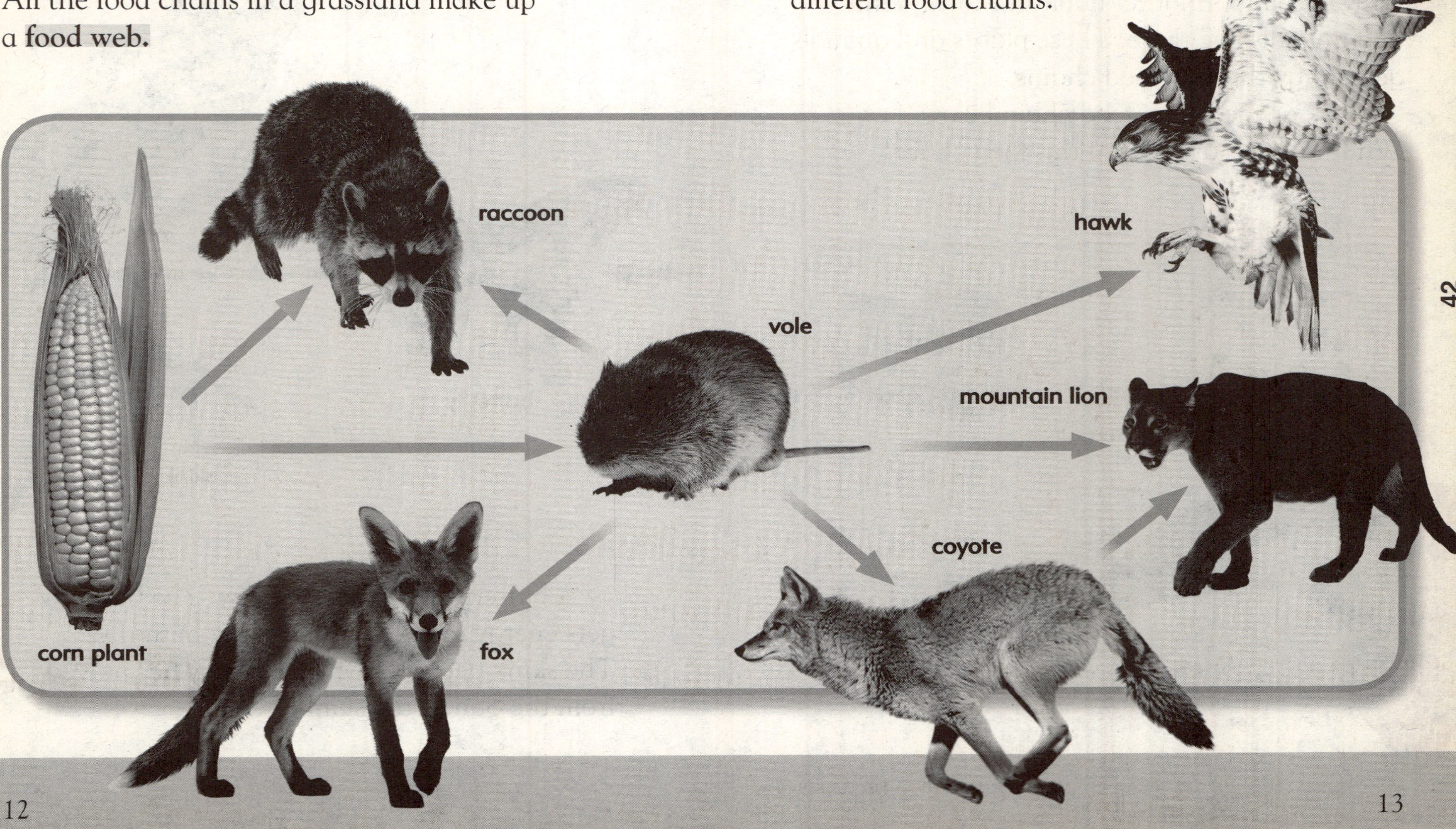

Science

Growing
and Changing

by Christian Downey

Genre	Comprehension Skill	Text Features	Science Content
Nonfiction	Infer	• Labels • Glossary	Living Things

Scott Foresman Science 2.4

PEARSON
Scott Foresman

DK

scottforesman.com

ISBN 0-328-13779-0

90000

9 780328 137794

What did you learn?

1. How does a tortoise grow?

2. How does a sunflower seed grow?

3. **Writing** in Science Young deer are called fawns. Write to explain how fawns are different from their parents. Use words from the book as you write.

4. **Infer** If you found a deer with antlers, what could you infer about its age?

Vocabulary

germinate
life cycle
nymph
seed coat
seedling

Picture Credits
Every effort has been made to secure permission and provide appropriate credit for photographic material.
The publisher deeply regrets any omission and pledges to correct errors called to its attention in subsequent editions.

Photo locators denoted as follows: Top (T), Center (C), Bottom (B), Left (L), Right (R), Background (Bkgd).

3 Anthony Bannister; Gallo Images/Corbis; 4 Anthony Bannister; Gallo Images/Corbis; 7 (TC) ©Jerry Young/DK Images;
8 ©Jerry Young/DK Images; 18 (CR) Stephen Haywood/DK Images; 19 (L)Willard Clay/Getty Images;
20 Walter Hodges/Getty Images.

Unless otherwise acknowledged, all photographs are the copyright © of Dorling Kindersley, a division of Pearson.

ISBN: 0-328-13779-0

Glossary

germinate	to begin to grow
life cycle	the way a living thing grows and changes
nymph	a young insect that has no wings
seed coat	a hard outer covering that protects a seed
seedling	a young plant

Growing and Changing

by Christian Downey

These toy animals are not living things.
They do not grow and change. They cannot
move. They do not eat or drink water. They
cannot be parents.

Children may look like other people in their
family. They may look like their brothers and
sisters. They may also look different in some
ways. How does this boy look different from his
mother? How do they look alike?

People Can Be Different

People have different hair colors. People have different skin colors. People have different eye colors. How are these children alike and different?

Tortoises Grow And Change

Plants and animals are living things. Living things grow and change. They need food and water. Some living things can move. Living things can be parents.

This tortoise is a living thing. It grows and changes.

Tortoises Start as Eggs

Tortoises live on land. They lay their eggs in a hole in the soil. They cover the hole.

People get bigger as they grow. Their teeth change. They grow taller. Some people's hair may become gray or white. Some people may get wrinkles.

People Grow And Change

People change in different ways as they grow. A baby will grow into a child. A child will grow to be an adult. An adult will grow to be an elderly person.

The eggs stay under the earth for some time. One day they hatch.

Young tortoises have an egg tooth. It helps them break out of the egg. When they grow up their egg tooth falls off.

Life Cycle of a Tortoise

A **life cycle** is how a living thing grows and changes. See the tortoise life cycle below.

Young Plants And Their Parents

Young plants can be like their parents or they can be different. They can be the same shape and color. Many plants grow bigger as they get older. How are these plants the same? How are they different?

Roots grow down and a stem grows up.
Fully grown sunflowers make seeds. Some seeds
will grow into new plants.

A seedling grows into a sunflower plant.

A Grown Tortoise

One day this adult tortoise will lay eggs and begin a new life cycle.

Life Cycle Of
A Sunflower

Sunflowers grow from seeds. A seed contains a tiny plant and food. Each sunflower seed has a **seed coat.** It keeps the seed safe. Seeds need water and air to grow. When sunflower seeds **germinate,** or grow, the seed coat bursts open. A tiny **seedling** comes out.

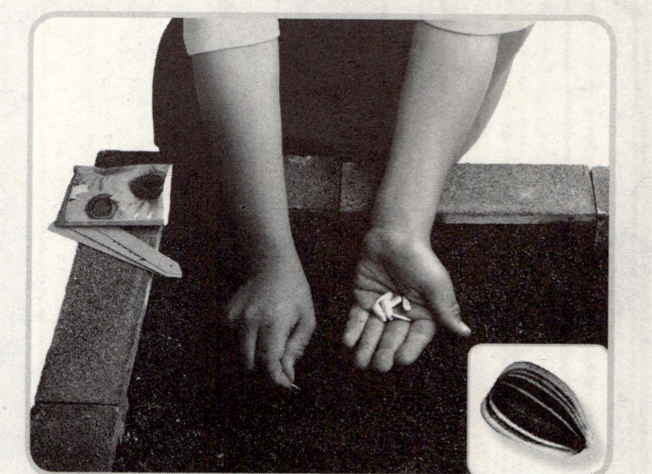

A sunflower seed gets planted.

The seed germinates.

This yellow duckling is covered with soft feathers called down. When it grows up its feathers will change.

Life Cycle Of A Ladybug

ladybug

Insects have life cycles. Young insects are called **nymphs.** Nymphs have no wings. They shed their outside covering as they grow.

From Egg to Adult

A ladybug is an insect.
Ladybugs have a life cycle.

Young Animals And their Parents

Young animals can look like their parents in shape and color. They also look different in some ways.

lioness and cub

This lion cub is smaller than its parent.

A young kangaroo rides in its mother's pouch. When it grows up it can move alone.

kangaroo and joey

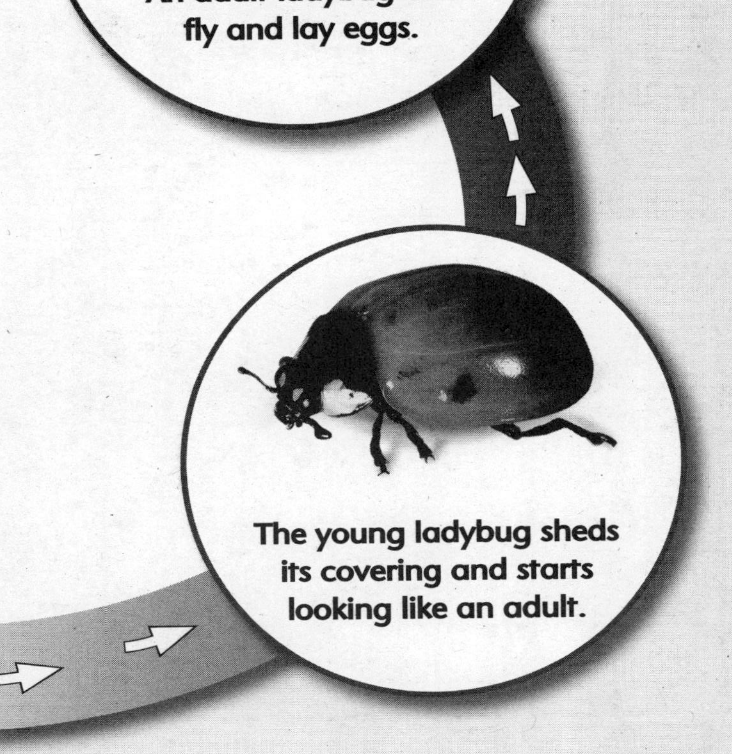

Life Cycle of a Deer

Deer are mammals. A young mammal grows inside its mother. It drinks milk from its mother. Young deer are called fawns.

When fawns grow up they can have fawns of their own. The adult deer in this picture can have fawns of their own.

The Earth

by Carol Levine

Genre	Comprehension Skill	Text Features	Science Content
Nonfiction	Picture Clues	• Call Outs • Captions • Labels • Glossary	Natural Resources

Scott Foresman Science 2.5

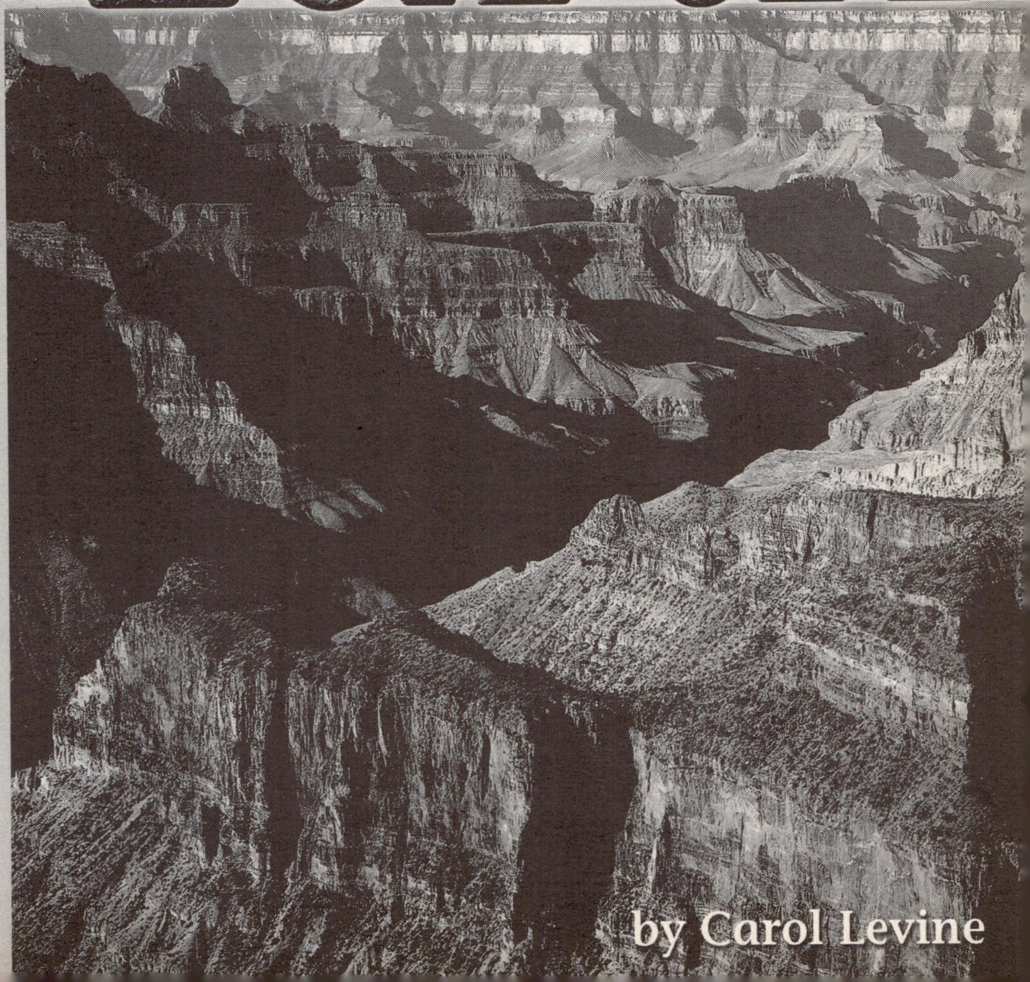

What did you learn?

Vocabulary

boulder
erosion
minerals
natural resource
pollution
recycle
sand
weathering

1. Where is water found on Earth?

2. What are rocks made of?

3. **Writing** in Science There are different kinds of soil. Write to explain the ways soil can be different. Use words from the book as you write.

4. **Picture Clues** What does the picture on page 14 show about the way weathering works on rocks?

ISBN: 0-328-13782-0

Glossary

boulder	a very large rock
erosion	when rocks or soil are moved by water or wind
minerals	nonliving materials that come from the Earth
natural resource	a useful material that comes from the Earth
pollution	when something harmful is added to the land, air, or water
recycle	to change something so it can be used again
sand	tiny pieces of rock
weathering	the breaking apart and changing of rocks by ice, wind, and rain

The Earth

by Carol Levine

PEARSON
Scott Foresman

DK

The Earth's Natural Resources

Our planet is rich in many ways. We use these riches every day. Scientists call these riches **natural resources.** We need to take care of the Earth and the things it provides for us.

Earth is full of natural resources. We need to protect them and use them with care. What can you do to help?

Sometimes people make changes to the Earth that hurt living things. Animals and plants lose their homes when people build where they live.

A refuge is a place where animals and plants can be safe. People are not allowed to live in refuges. People can protect living things by creating refuges.

Some natural resources, such as oil and coal, can be used up. Other natural resources, such as trees, can be replaced when they are used. Some natural resources cannot be used up. Sunlight and air cannot be used up.

Water and Air

Living things need water. There is fresh water on Earth. It is found in ponds, rivers, and lakes. There is also salt water. It is found in oceans and seas.

Plants, animals, and people use water in many ways. Think of all the ways you use water.

When trees are lost, animals can lose their homes. People can plant new trees. It takes a long time for trees to grow big. Even so, it is important to plant new trees. This helps the living things of the forest.

Protecting Plants And Animals

Earth changes all the time. Forests change. Sometimes people cause forests to change. Forests change when people cut down trees.

People do not make all the changes. Fires and storms change forests when they kill trees.

Living things need air too. Air is all around us. Wind is air moving. We cannot see air, even when it moves.

Animals and plants need air to live. People need air to breathe.

Water and air are natural resources.

Rocks and Soil

Rocks are a natural resource. Rocks can be different sizes. Rocks can be different shapes and colors too.

People use rocks for many things. We use them to make roads and buildings.

To **recycle** means to change something so it can be used again. We make less trash when we recycle. Lots of things can be recycled. Can you think of things to recycle?

Another way to help make less pollution is to reuse things many times. Instead of using a new lunch bag every day, we could use the same lunch box many times. This makes less trash.

Large rocks are called **boulders.** Rocks are broken down by wind, rain, and ice. **Sand** is made up of many small rocks.

gold

Gold and garnets are
used to make jewelry.

garnet

Getting rid of all the trash we make is hard.
Making less trash is the first step. Less trash
will mean less pollution.

People can help make less pollution. Trash is
a big part of pollution. When people pick up their
trash, they are helping to stop pollution.

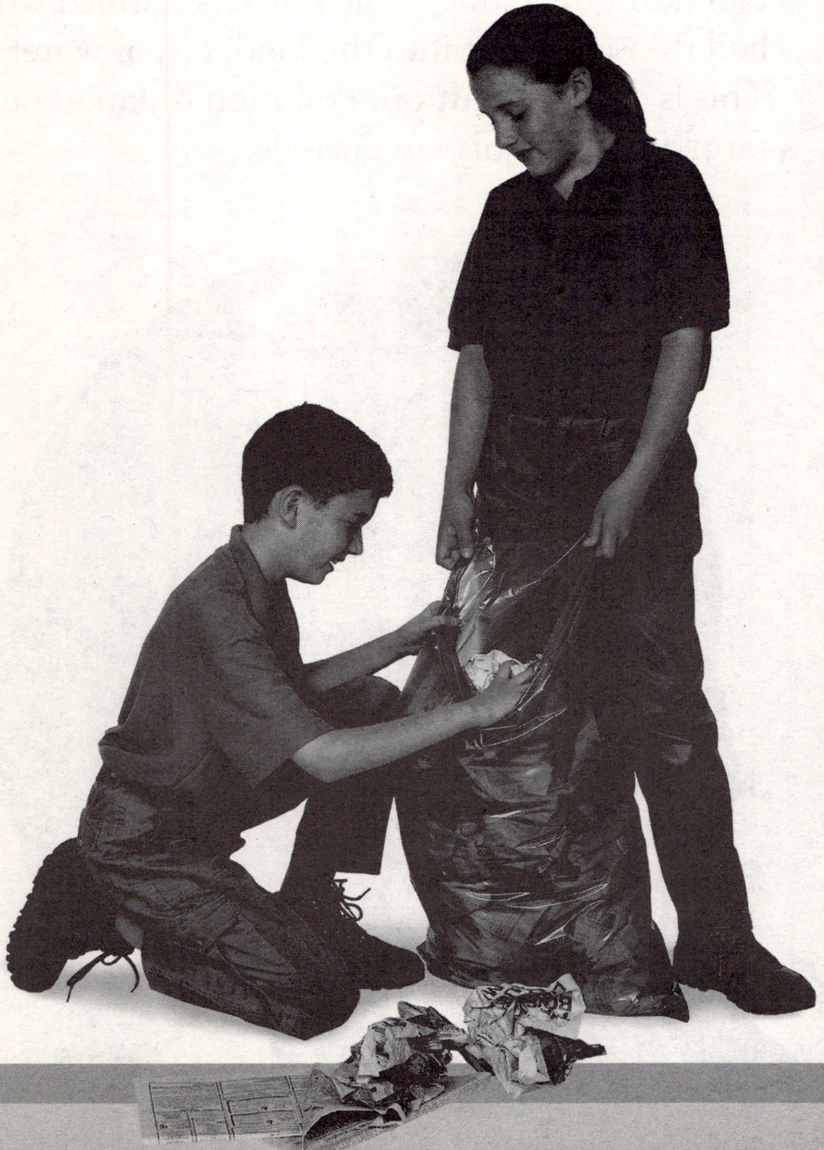

Rocks are made of **minerals.** Minerals are
nonliving things. They are natural resources.
People use minerals all the time. Gold, silver,
and iron are some minerals we use.

iron

**Iron is used to
make bridges.**

Soil covers most of the land on Earth.
This natural resource is made of
many parts. Clay, sand,
humus, air, and water
are in soil. Soil is a
mixture of these parts.

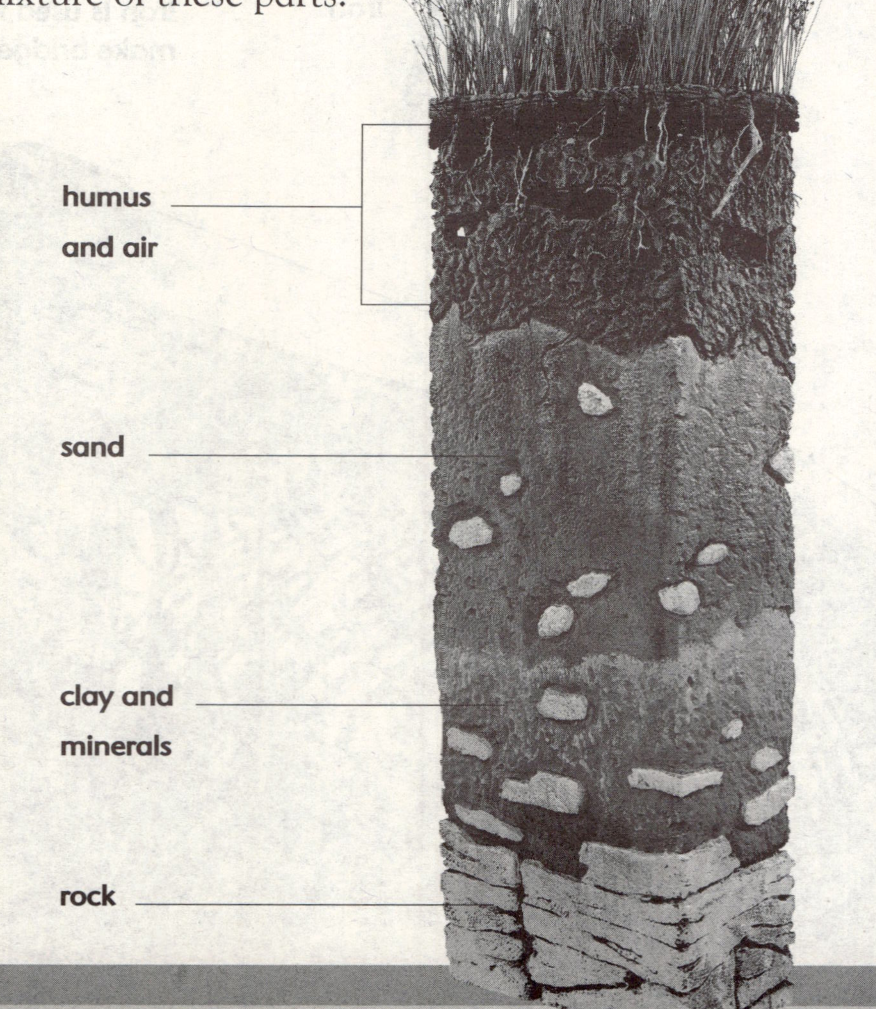

Pollution

People can change the Earth. Some changes
can harm the planet. The Earth is harmed when
bad things are put into the land, air, or water.
This is called **pollution.** Pollution is dangerous
for plants, animals, and people.

Weathering also changes the Earth.
Weathering is when ice, wind, and rain break
and change rocks. Weathering happens slowly.

There are different kinds of soil. Soil can be
different colors. Soil can feel hard, crumbly,
or soft. Soil can be wet or dry. Different plants
grow in different soil. Some plants
like salty soil. Potatoes grow well
in red-colored soil that
has lots of iron.

Plants

Plants are a natural resource.
Plants have different parts.
People use parts of plants
in many ways. We use wood
from trees to build houses.
We use lots of plants
as food.

Erosion And Weathering

Earth changes all the time. Erosion and weathering change the Earth. **Erosion** is when water or wind moves the rocks or soil. Plants help stop erosion. Their roots hold on to the soil.

Earth's Weather

by Christine Wolf

Genre	Comprehension Skill	Text Features	Science Content
Nonfiction	Draw Conclusions	• Captions • Diagrams • Glossary	Weather

Scott Foresman Science 2.6

ISBN 0-328-13785-5

9 780328 137855

90000

PEARSON

Scott
Foresman

scottforesman.com

What did you learn?

1. What is one difference between fall and spring?

2. What is the difference between hibernating and migrating? How are these two behaviors similar?

3. **Writing** in Science Sometimes wet weather can be dangerous. In your own words, write to tell about the different kinds of dangerous weather. Use words from the book as you write.

4. **Draw Conclusions** The ground is wet. The air is cool. There are tulips poking through the soil. Baby geese are sitting near their mother in the green grass. What season do you think it might be?

Picture Credits
Every effort has been made to secure permission and provide appropriate credit for photographic material. The publisher deeply regrets any omission and pledges to correct errors called to its attention in subsequent editions.

Photo locators denoted as follows: Top (T), Center (C), Bottom (B), Left (L), Right (R), Background (Bkgd).

Opener: Digital Vision; 2 (R) Digital Vision; 3 Digital Vision; 4 Digital Vision; 5 (T, B) Joanna Van Gruisen/Ardea; 8 (TR, BR) Getty Images; 9 (TL, BL) Getty Images; 10 (R, BL) Getty Images; 11 (TR) Digital Vision; 12 (R) Getty Images; 14 (R) Getty Images; 15 (TR) William H. Mullins/Photo Researchers, Inc.; 16 (R, Bkgd) Getty Images; 18 Digital Vision; 20 Digital Vision; 21 Getty Images; 22 Getty Images.

Unless otherwise acknowledged, all photographs are the copyright © of Dorling Kindersley, a division of Pearson.

ISBN: 0-328-13785-5

Copyright © Pearson Education, Inc.

All Rights Reserved. Printed in the United States of America. The blackline masters in this publication are designed for use with appropriate equipment to reproduce copies for classroom use only. Scott Foresman grants permission to classroom teachers to reproduce from these masters.

2 3 4 5 6 7 8 9 10 V004 13 12 11 10 09 08 07 06 05

Glossary

Term	Definition
condense	to change from water vapor to water droplets
evaporate	to change from water to water vapor
hibernate	to hide away and sleep through winter
hurricane	a very strong storm that starts over the ocean
lightning	a flash of light in the sky
migrate	to move to a warmer place when winter is coming
tornado	a circling column of air
water cycle	the movement of water from Earth to the sky and back again

Earth's Weather

by Christine Wolf

What is weather?

Weather happens because of changes in Earth's temperature. Days can be hot or cold, wet or dry. Different kinds of clouds and wind are also a part of weather.

When a hurricane is coming, people who live near the beach move away from the water so they can stay away from huge waves. People board up windows and bring inside things that might fly around.

Staying Safe
In a Hurricane

When many thunderstorms join together, a **hurricane** may form. Heavy rains fall during hurricanes. Strong winds blow and knock down buildings and trees.

What makes weather wet or dry?

Rain, hail, and snow are kinds of wet weather. Clouds are made of lots of water droplets and tiny bits of ice. The clouds get big and heavy.

When the air is warm the droplets can fall to the ground as rain. When the air is cold they may fall down as sleet or snow.

Some places do not get a lot of rain. These places have very dry weather. When there is not enough rain for plants and animals to live, it is called a drought.

Tornadoes can be unexpected. If you are ever caught in a tornado you should find shelter indoors. You should stay in the basement or under the stairs. Keep away from windows, water, and metal objects.

Staying Safe
In a Tornado

Tornadoes are made up
of strong winds that move in
a circle. Air inside a tornado
acts like a giant straw.
Everything in a tornado's path
gets sucked up into the sky.

Some places are wet and green in winter.
In the summer they can be dry and brown.

The Water Cycle

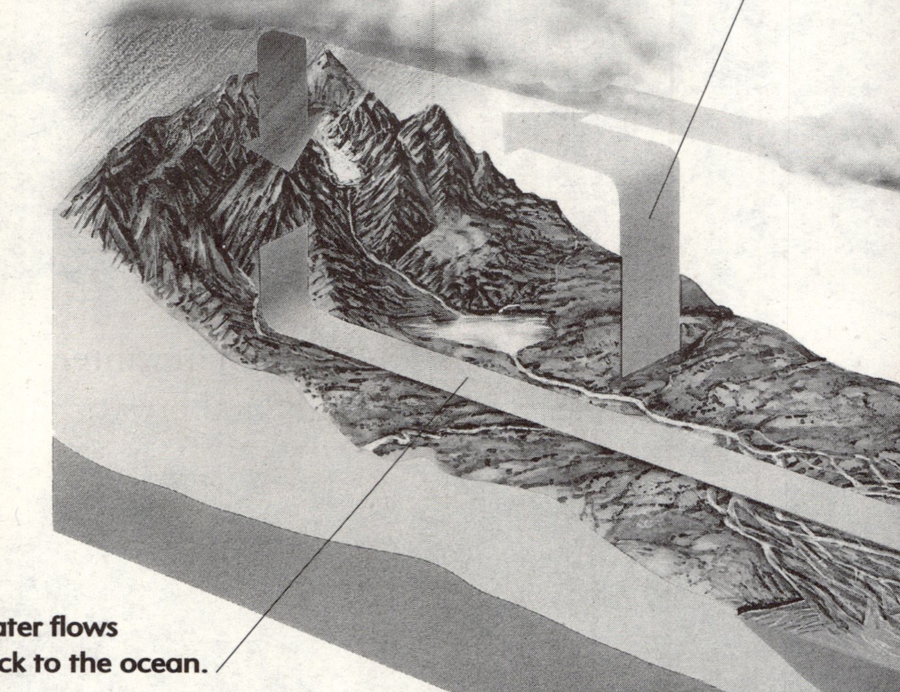

The wheel on a bicycle goes around in a circle. Water in Earth's **water cycle** also goes round and round.

Staying Safe In A Thunderstorm

Staying safe from lightning means finding shelter in a building. It also helps to stay away from water, metal objects, and trees.

Dangerous Weather

Sometimes wet weather can be dangerous. Thunderstorms often form on hot summer days.

They can bring heavy rain, hail, thunder, and lightning.

Lightning is a flash of light in the sky. Thunder is the sound that follows lightning.

Earth's water keeps moving between the oceans, the sky, and the land. Water **evaporates** from the ocean and rises to form clouds.

The water vapor in clouds gets cold and changes, or **condenses,** back to water droplets. The water droplets fall back to the ground.

Rain gathers in rivers and runs to oceans. The Sun heats the oceans and the cycle begins again.

The Four Seasons

Many parts of the world have four seasons. They are spring, summer, fall, and winter. Each season has its own weather.

spring

fall

Some animals hibernate in winter. **Hibernate** means to hide away and sleep. Animals that hibernate fatten up so their bodies can stay warm as they sleep. What is winter like where you live?

80

Winter

Winter is the coldest season. In many places, snow falls, lakes and ponds freeze, and icicles form. Winter has the fewest hours of daylight. The Sun is low in the sky.

The four seasons together last one year. In each season days can be longer or shorter. Animals and plants behave differently in each season too.

Spring

Spring is the season of change and growth. Often, spring has rainy days and cool nights. Small plants begin to grow in spring.

Other animals, such as Canada geese, travel, or **migrate,** to warmer places. What is fall like where you live?

Fall

In fall the temperature cools down. There are fewer hours of daylight than in summer. Leaves may change color, and some leaves fall off the trees.

In the fall many animals begin to prepare for the winter. Some animals, such as squirrels, gather and store food.

You may see new green leaves on trees. Many baby animals are born in the spring. Lots of flowers can bloom. What is spring like where you live?

Summer

Summer is often hot and sunny. Summer has more hours of daylight than spring. The Sun is high in the sky. Many people like to be outside in the summer.

Baby animals grow up in the summer. Many fruits and vegetables get ripe in the summer. What is summer like where you live?

Dinosaur Fossils

by Kim Borland

Genre	Comprehension Skill	Text Features	Science Content
Nonfiction	Retell	• Labels • Glossary	Fossils and Dinosaurs

Scott Foresman Science 2.7

What did you learn?

1. Which is the biggest dinosaur ever found? Where was it found?

2. What is a fossil?

3. **Writing** in Science
Paleontologists study living things from long ago. What do you think a paleontologist's day might be like? Write to tell your ideas. Use words from the book as you write.

4. Retell On page 4, the author explains how a dinosaur fossil might form. Using your own words, retell how this might happen.

Picture Credits
Every effort has been made to secure permission and provide appropriate credit for photographic material.
The publisher deeply regrets any omission and pledges to correct errors called to its attention in subsequent editions.

Photo locators denoted as follows: Top (T), Center (C), Bottom (B), Left (L), Right (R), Background (Bkgd).

5 ©Jonathan Blair/Corbis; 8 Bettmann/Corbis.

Unless otherwise acknowledged, all photographs are the copyright © of Dorling Kindersley, a division of Pearson.

ISBN: 0-328-13788-X

Copyright © Pearson Education, Inc.

All Rights Reserved. Printed in the United States of America. The blackline masters in this publication are designed for use with appropriate equipment to reproduce copies for classroom use only. Scott Foresman grants permission to classroom teachers to reproduce from these masters.

2 3 4 5 6 7 8 9 10 V004 13 12 11 10 09 08 07 06 05

Glossary

dinosaurs	extinct animals that lived long ago
extinct	a plant or animal that no longer lives on Earth
fossil	a print or remains of a plant or animal that lived long ago
paleontologist	a scientist who studies fossils

Dinosaur Fossils

by Kim Borland

Millions of years ago, **dinosaurs** roamed the Earth. Dinosaurs of all shapes and sizes lived together on the land.

Triceratops

Diplodocus

Are there even bigger dinosaur fossils to be found? Paleontologists are always looking for new fossil clues. Each discovery tells us more about how these animals lived. So keep your eyes open. Maybe the next big dinosaur discovery will be yours!

**Tyrannosaurus rex was 39 feet long.
Gigantosaurus was 45 feet long.
How much longer was Gigantosaurus?**

The dinosaurs disappeared from the Earth before there were any people to see them, tell about them, or draw pictures of them. So how do we know so much about them? Let's find out!

New Discoveries

For many years paleontologists thought T. rex was the largest meat-eating dinosaur. In 1993 a paleontologist made an amazing discovery. He found the fossils of a Gigantosaurus in Argentina. This dinosaur was even bigger than T. rex!

Learning About the Past

Everything we know about dinosaurs comes from fossils. A **fossil** can be a very old bone, a tooth, a footprint, or even a piece of skin.

A **paleontologist** is a scientist who studies fossils. These paleontologists are studying the fossils of a Tyrannosaurus rex, T. rex for short, that lived more than 67 million years ago.

How did dinosaur fossils form?

Paleontologists think this dinosaur fell into a river when it died. It was buried under soft sand and mud. When the river dried up, the sand and mud turned into rock. Over millions of years, this dinosaur's bones turned into rock too. These are the fossils we find today.

By studying the fossils of the Triceratops (try-SE-ruh-tops), paleontologists know that its babies were born with three horns. The three horns got bigger as the dinosaur grew older.

Fossils of baby Protoceratops show that it was born with its head frill.

Studying Dinosaurs

By studying the fossils of a Barosaurus (ba-ruh-SAW-ruhs), paleontologists know that this dinosaur had a long, strong neck. The dinosaur could stand on its back legs and reach the highest trees. It used its tiny teeth to pull leaves off branches.

This paleontologist is looking at the fossil skull of a small kind of T. rex, called an Albertosaurus.

What can we learn from fossils?

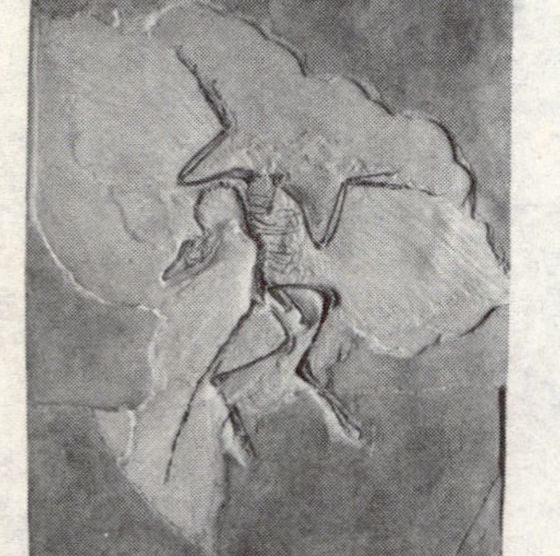

This rock contains a bird fossil.

Fossils are like a journal. They tell us what the Earth was like in the past. By studying fossils, paleontologists learn interesting things about different dinosaurs.

Paleontologists know that some dinosaurs were as tall as buildings. Some were as small as chickens. Some dinosaurs ate leaves and fruits. Some ate other animals.

By studying dinosaur tracks, paleontologists know that some dinosaurs moved slowly on four legs. Some raced on two legs.

Triceratops

These are dinosaur footprints.

Animals and plants that no longer live on Earth are **extinct.** Dinosaurs disappeared from the Earth a long time ago. They are extinct. For some reason the dinosaurs' habitat could no longer meet their needs. Some paleontologists think that this is because their habitat changed.

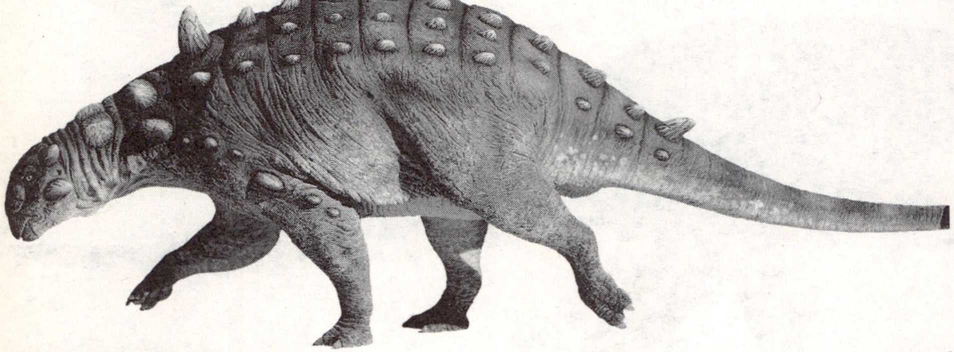

Euoplocephalus

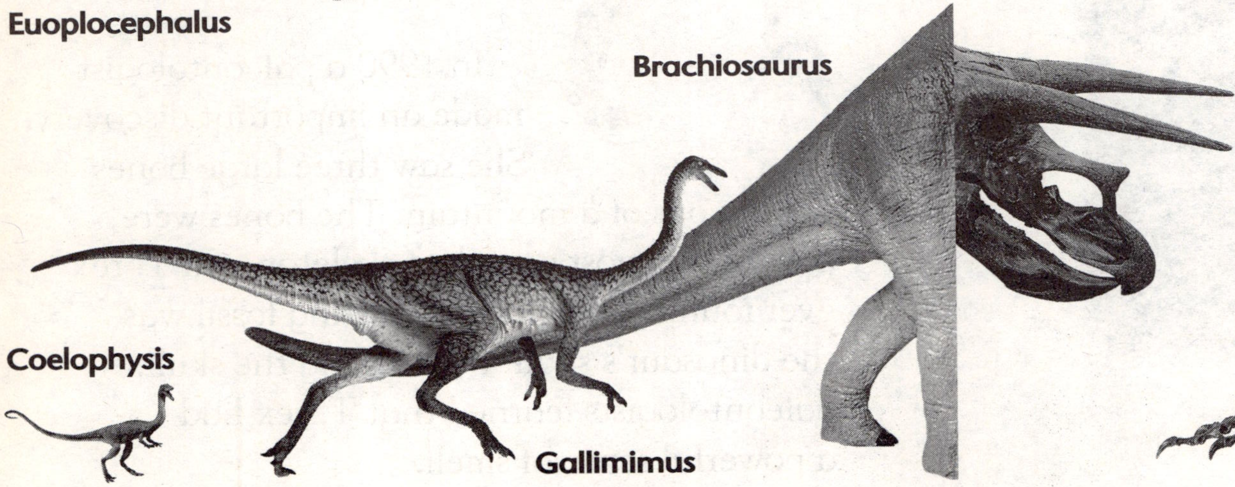

Brachiosaurus

Coelophysis

Gallimimus

What did dinosaurs really look like? How big were they? How did their bodies work? What did they eat? How did they move? Paleontologists ask these questions as they study dinosaur fossils.

fossil of Saltasaurus skin

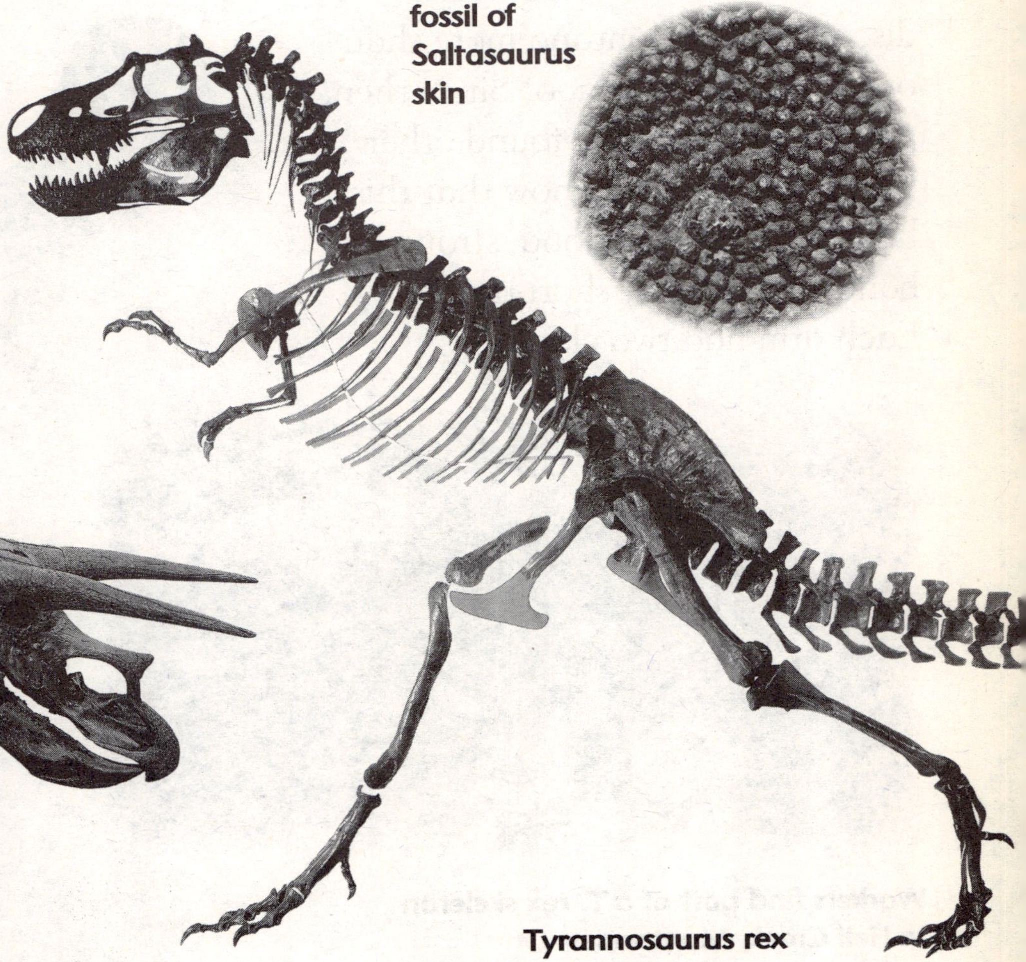

Tyrannosaurus rex

What were dinosaurs like?

The first T. rex fossil was discovered in Montana more than one hundred years ago! Since then, paleontologists have found other T. rex fossils. They know that this huge dinosaur had long, strong leg bones. It had very short arms. Each arm had two claws.

T. rex skull

Workers find part of a T. rex skeleton in Hell Creek, Montana.

In 1990 a paleontologist made an important discovery. She saw three large bones poking out of a mountain. The bones were part of the most complete skeleton of a T. rex ever found. The most interesting fossil was the dinosaur's skull. By studying the skull, paleontologists learned that T. rex had a powerful sense of smell.

Matter

by Kim Fields

Genre	Comprehension Skill	Text Features	Science Content
Nonfiction	Draw Conclusions	• Captions • Glossary	Matter

Scott Foresman Science 2.8

What did you learn?

1. What are some properties of matter that you can observe by seeing?

2. How is a solid different from a gas?

3. **Writing** in Science Water can change from a gas into a liquid. Write to explain how this happens. Use the words *water vapor, gas,* and *liquid* as you write.

4. **Draw Conclusions** What could you do to change milk into a solid?

Picture Credits
Every effort has been made to secure permission and provide appropriate credit for photographic material.
The publisher deeply regrets any omission and pledges to correct errors called to its attention in subsequent editions.

Unless otherwise acknowledged, all photographs are the copyright © of Dorling Kindersley, a division of Pearson.

ISBN: 0-328-13791-X

Copyright © Pearson Education, Inc.

All Rights Reserved. Printed in the United States of America. The blackline masters in this publication are designed for use with appropriate equipment to reproduce copies for classroom use only. Scott Foresman grants permission to classroom teachers to reproduce from these masters.

2 3 4 5 6 7 8 9 10 V004 13 12 11 10 09 08 07 06 05

Glossary

gas	matter that has mass and takes the shape of its container
liquid	matter that has mass and takes the shape of its container
mass	the amount of matter in an object
mixture	two or more things with different properties that can be separated
property	something about matter that you can observe with your senses
solid	matter that has mass and its own size and shape
states of matter	the different forms matter can take: solid, liquid, or gas

Matter

by Kim Fields

Matter

All things are made of matter.
Matter has mass and takes up space.
Think about your bedroom. Your bed,
clothes, and toys are
made of matter.

Heating can change
a liquid into a gas.

When you light a candle,
the candle wax gets hot.
It melts and turns into
liquid wax.

The liquid wax gets
hotter and turns into
a gas. This is why
the candle gets smaller!

Heating Matter

Heating can change a solid into a liquid. Chocolate is a solid. When chocolate is heated, it melts. Melted chocolate is a liquid.

Even things you cannot see are made of matter. Air is a kind of matter.

All things made of matter have mass. **Mass** is how much matter is in an object.

Matter is made of tiny parts. You can see the tiny parts of matter through a microscope.

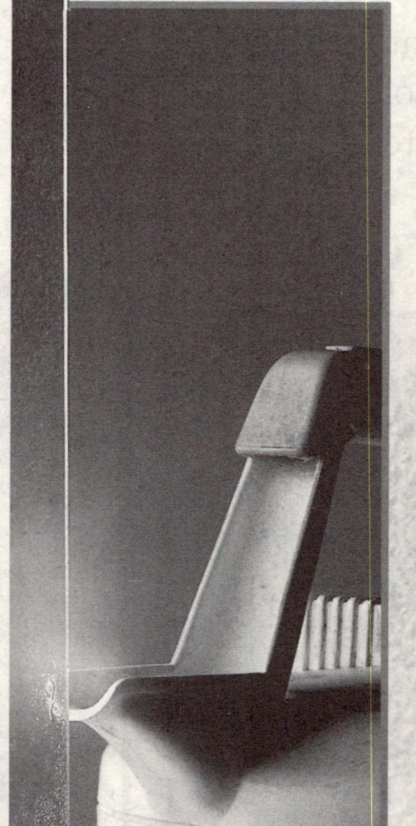

Water vapor from a kettle touches cold glass and changes into drops of water.

Water can also change from a liquid to a solid. This liquid rain changed to solid ice when it got very cold.

Rainwater drips from the roof and freezes. It changes into solid ice.

Properties
of Matter

Matter has different properties.
You can observe a **property** using
your senses. Some properties are
color, size, shape, and weight.

**One property of matter is weight.
Which of these is light?
Which of these is heavy?**

Air contains water vapor. Water vapor is a gas.
Water vapor can change from a gas to a liquid.
When water vapor touches something cold,
it changes to liquid drops of water.

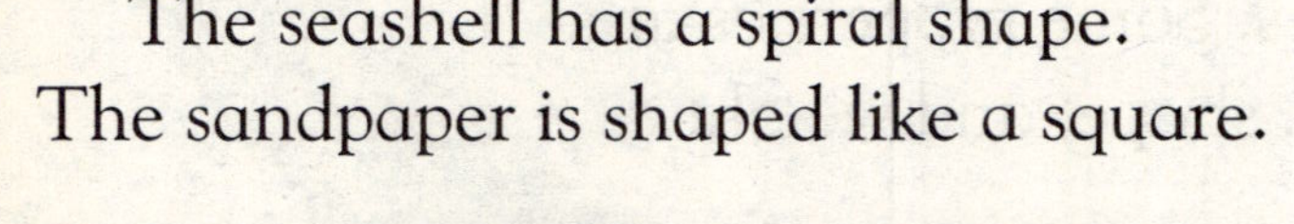

You can see and touch some properties of matter.

Matter can feel smooth or rough. This seashell feels smooth. Sandpaper feels rough.

The seashell has a spiral shape. The sandpaper is shaped like a square.

Cooling Matter

Fruit juice is liquid matter. It can change when you cool it. Pour juice into molds. Put the molds into the freezer. The juice in each mold will turn into a frozen treat. Then it will be a solid.

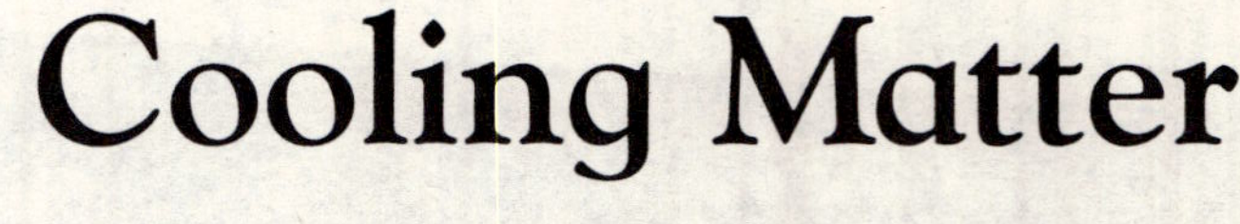

Mixing with Water

Water is used to make some mixtures. You can separate these mixtures in different ways. Put oil and water together. The water sinks and the oil floats.

Mix sugar and water. If you heat this mixture, the water can separate by evaporating.

Oil floats on water.

Sugar mixes with water.

Another property of matter is size. This beach ball is big. The golf ball is small.

Color is a property of matter. What colors can you see on this beach ball?

States of Matter

The three **states of matter** are solid, liquid, and gas.

Solids

A **solid** has its own shape and size. A solid also has mass and takes up space.

A table is a solid. Your pencils and erasers are also solids. They all have a size, shape, and weight.

You can separate a mixture into its parts. Each marble can be taken out one at a time. You can separate the yellow marbles from the green marbles.

Mixing and Separating Matter

A **mixture** is something made of two or more things. The things you put in a mixture do not change.

These marbles are a mixture of colors. The marbles are also a mixture of sizes.

You can measure the size of some solids with a ruler.

A notebook is made of solid matter. You can find out how long, tall, and wide it is.

Liquids

A **liquid** is a kind of matter without a shape. A liquid takes the shape of the container that holds it. Liquids have mass and take up space.

Matter can change in shape. It can become round or square. It can become flat or bumpy.

You can change dough into many shapes.

Changing Matter

There are many ways to change matter.
Matter can change in size.
It can get bigger or smaller.

The size of matter can change. Take some bites out of an apple. Now the apple is a different size!

Milk is a liquid. It takes the shape of the carton or jug that holds it. Pour milk into a glass. Now it takes the shape of the glass.

A liquid can be measured using a measuring cup. You can pour milk into a measuring cup to find its volume. The amount of space a liquid takes up is called its volume.

A measuring cup measures the amount of space taken up by a liquid.

Gases

Gas is also a kind of matter. Gas can change size and shape. Gas takes the size and the shape of whatever holds it. Gas also has mass.

The air you blow into a balloon is made of gases. You cannot see the gases. They take up space, but they have no shape of their own.

What is Energy?

by Christian Downey

Genre	Comprehension Skill	Text Features	Science Content
Nonfiction	Infer	• Call Outs • Captions • Labels • Glossary	Energy

Scott Foresman Science 2.9

PEARSON
Scott Foresman

DK

ISBN 0-328-13794-4

scottforesman.com

What did you learn?

1. How do plants and animals get energy?

2. What are some kinds of energy?

3. **Writing** in Science Shadows change during the day. In your own words, write to explain why this happens.

4. **Infer** What can you infer about someone wearing dark blue clothing on a hot, sunny day? How will that person feel?

Picture Credits
Every effort has been made to secure permission and provide appropriate credit for photographic material.
The publisher deeply regrets any omission and pledges to correct errors called to its attention in subsequent editions.

Photo locators denoted as follows: Top (T), Center (C), Bottom (B), Left (L), Right (R), Background (Bkgd).

11 (BR) ©Comstock Inc.; 12 Sally Lancaster/Alamy Images; 14 (CL) Getty Images; 19 (BR) Getty Images; 21 (BR) ©Judith Miller/Branksome Antiques/DK Images; 23 (TL) Getty Images.

Scott Foresman/Dorling Kindersley would also like to thank: 1 Pitt Rivers Museum, Oxford/DK Images; 4 Phil Farrand/DK Images; 5 (TR) NASA/DK Images; 14 Pitt Rivers Museum, Oxford/DK Images; 15 Jane Bull/DK Images.

Unless otherwise acknowledged, all photographs are the copyright © of Dorling Kindersley, a division of Pearson.

ISBN: 0-328-13794-4

Copyright © Pearson Education, Inc.

Glossary

conductor	a material that lets heat move easily through it
energy	anything that can do work or cause change
fuel	something that is burned to make heat
reflect	to bounce back from a surface
shadow	a dark area that forms when a light source is blocked
solar energy	heat and light from the Sun
source	a place from which something comes

What is Energy?

by Christian Downey

PEARSON Scott Foresman · DK

Energy

You use energy all the time. You use energy when you talk. You use energy when you eat.

Anything that can do work or cause change has **energy.**

When you throw a ball, you give the ball the energy of motion.

All living things need and use energy. Energy comes from many different sources. The most important source of energy is the Sun.

Did you use light or heat from the Sun today? Did you use electricity? Pay attention to the sources of energy you use. Energy is all around us!

Other Kinds
of Energy

Some other kinds of energy are
motion, wind, sound, and electricity.

You use energy when you walk, run, or
play sports. You use energy when you think.
You even use energy when you sleep!

**A kite uses
wind energy
to move.**

**This drum can make sound.
Sound is a kind of energy.**

Solar Energy

Earth gets energy from the Sun. Energy from the Sun is called **solar energy.** Solar energy is heat and light. People can use the Sun's energy to make things work.

Without the Sun, Earth would be dark and cold.

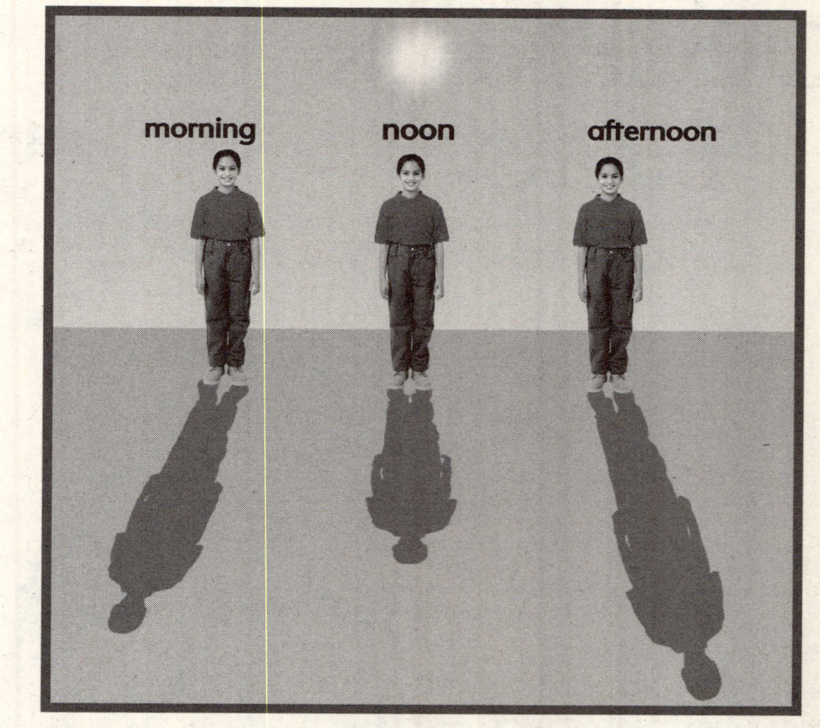

Shadows change during the day. In the early morning, light from the Sun makes long shadows. At noon the Sun shines directly above us. Shadows are very short. The sunlight cannot easily be blocked. In the late afternoon, long shadows can be made again. It becomes easier to block the sunlight.

This sundial works by using changing shadows.

Shadows

A **shadow** is made when something blocks
a source of light. You can make a shadow
by blocking light with your body. You can play
with shadows using a flashlight.

solar-powered calculator

The calculator above uses the Sun's energy
to work. The solar panel traps the solar energy.
The car below also uses the Sun's energy to work.

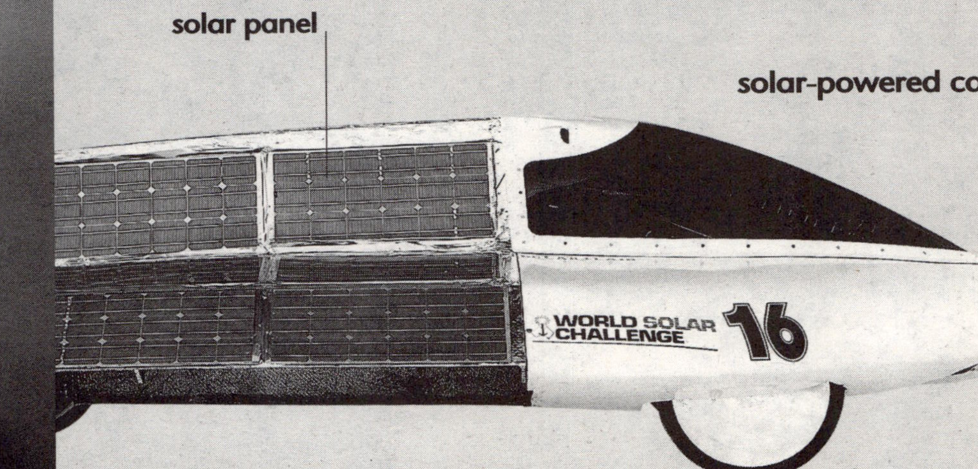

solar-powered car

Living Things Use Energy

All living things need energy. Green plants use energy to live, grow, and make food. Green plants get energy from the Sun. They make food using sunlight, air, and water.

Light reflects off light colors. The next time you are hot, wear something white. You will feel cooler.

Light does not reflect as much off dark colors. If you wear something dark on a hot, sunny day, you will get even hotter!

Light-colored clothes reflect light from the Sun.

The light we see is called white light. But it is made up of many different colors. This prism is bending the sunlight. The light becomes separated into its colors. How many colors can you see?

Raindrops can act like prisms to make rainbows. The raindrops bend the light and separate it into its colors.

Animals use energy to live, grow, and move. Animals get energy from food. Some animals get energy from eating green plants. People use energy too.

All living things need energy to live.

People Get Energy from Food

Food gives us energy. When you get energy from food, you can work, play, and grow. Different kinds of food keep your body healthy.

Light moves in straight lines. It can move through things that are clear. Light can move through glass or water.

Sometimes light hits an object it cannot go through. Light will bounce, or **reflect,** off the object.

A mirror is not clear.
Light cannot go through it.
Light reflects off a mirror.

Light

Light is a kind of energy.
Light can come from a candle,
a lamp, or the Sun. Most sources
of heat also give off light.

Candles and lamps
are sources of
light and heat.

There are five important food groups.
Your body needs food from all these groups.
If you eat too many sweets or foods from
one group, you may not stay healthy.

If you eat
healthful food,
you will have
lots of energy.

The Five
Food Groups

This picture shows
foods from the five
food groups. Which
foods did you eat today?

1 Meat, fish, eggs,
and dry beans help
your body grow.

2 Fruits have vitamins
and minerals that
your body needs.

3 Bread, rice, cereals,
and pasta give
your body energy.

Some materials are heat conductors.
A **conductor** is a material that allows heat
to pass easily through it. The cookie tray
in this picture is made of metal. Metal is
a conductor. The tray lets heat get to the
cookies. The oven mitts are not conductors.
Heat cannot move easily through them.

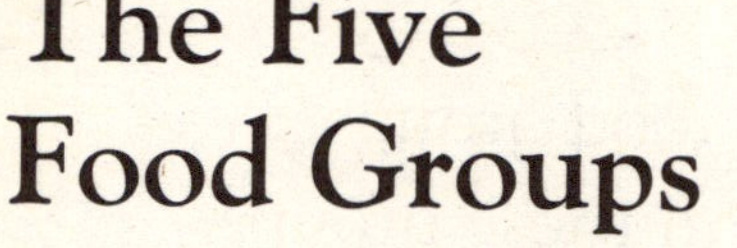

**Oven mitts can protect
our hands from heat
because they are not
good conductors.**

120

Heat Moves

Heat moves from hot places and objects to cooler places and objects. In this picture, heat is moving from the fire to the marshmallows.

121

Sources of Heat

A **source** is a place from which something comes. Heat can come from the Sun. The Sun is one source of heat.

Heat can come from other sources too. Heat can come from a stove. Heat can come from a fire.

A stove is a source of heat.

Some stoves use gas. Gas is a kind of fuel. A **fuel** is something that is burned to make heat. Wood, oil, and coal can also be used as fuel.

Exploring Forces and Motion

by Sasha Griffin

Genre	Comprehension Skill	Text Features	Science Content
Nonfiction	Put Things in Order	• Captions • Glossary	Forces and Motion

Scott Foresman Science 2.10

PEARSON
Scott Foresman

DK

ISBN 0-328-13797-9

9 780328 137978

scottforesman.com

What did you learn?

1. When do you need to use more force to move objects?

2. What are some simple machines, and what do they do?

3. **Writing** in Science Magnets can pull things toward them and push things away. Write to explain how they do this. Use words from the book as you write.

4. **Put Things in Order** Tell what happens in order when you throw a ball up in the air. Use the words *force* and *gravity*.

Picture Credits
Every effort has been made to secure permission and provide appropriate credit for photographic material.
The publisher deeply regrets any omission and pledges to correct errors called to its attention in subsequent editions.

Photo locators denoted as follows: Top (T), Center (C), Bottom (B), Left (L), Right (R), Background (Bkgd).

5 Getty Images; 8 (TL) ©AFP/Getty Images, (TR) ©Chapman/NewSport/Corbis; 12 (BR) Paul Hobson/Alamy Images.

Unless otherwise acknowledged, all photographs are the copyright © of Dorling Kindersley, a division of Pearson.

ISBN: 0-328-13797-9

Copyright © Pearson Education, Inc.

All Rights Reserved. Printed in the United States of America. The blackline masters in this publication are designed for use with appropriate equipment to reproduce copies for classroom use only. Scott Foresman grants permission to classroom teachers to reproduce from these masters.

2 3 4 5 6 7 8 9 10 V004 13 12 11 10 09 08 07 06 05

Glossary

attract	to pull toward
force	a push or pull that makes something move
friction	a force that slows or stops moving objects
gravity	a force that pulls things toward Earth's center
motion	the act of moving
repel	to push away
simple machine	a tool that has few or no moving parts
work	what happens when a force moves an object

Exploring Forces and Motion

by Sasha Griffin

How Objects Move

Objects move in many ways. We call the act of moving **motion.**

You can push a crayon across a piece of paper in a straight line or a zigzag motion.

You can move a tennis ball up and down. A Ferris wheel moves around in a circle.

What Magnets Attract

Magnets attract objects made of iron or steel. They do not attract all kinds of metal. A magnet will attract steel paper clips. It will not attract a gold ring. Gold is a different kind of metal.

Magnets do not attract things made of wood, plastic, or paper. Do you think a magnet will attract a crayon?

126

A magnet has two ends, or poles. We call one
end the north pole and the other the south pole.
A magnet's strongest push or pull is at the poles.
   Try putting two poles that are the same
together. The magnets will repel each other.
If you put the opposite poles together, the magnets
will attract each other.

You use force to throw a ball and
to make it change direction.

Force

We use **force** to move things. Force is
a push or pull that makes something move.
   Objects move in the direction they are
pushed or pulled. When the direction of
the force is changed, an object moves in
that different direction.

You can make an object move faster by using more force. The merry-go-round will move faster if the boy pushes harder. It takes more force to move heavy objects than light ones.

Would the boy need to use more force to push the merry-go-round when it is empty or when it is full of kids?

Magnets stick to a refrigerator because it is made of metal.

Magnets

Magnets are used in many ways. Magnets **attract** some types of metal. That means they pull some metal objects toward themselves. Magnets can push away, or **repel,** other magnets.

A magnet's force can move some objects without touching them.

Animal Body Parts

Some animals have body parts that work like simple machines.

A woodpecker pecks holes in tree trunks. Its beak is like a wedge.

Moles have front feet that they use like levers. They move dirt as they dig.

A woodpecker uses its beak like a wedge.

A mole uses its front feet like levers.

Gravity

When you throw something into the air, **gravity** will pull it down. Gravity is a force that pulls things toward the center of Earth.

What do you think will happen when these children jump up? Gravity will pull them back down.

Work

When a force moves an object, we call that **work.** No work is done when an object does not move. When you pick up a pencil, you are using force and doing work.

A bicycle has two wheels and two axles.

A wheel and axle make a simple machine. When you put force on one wheel, the axle turns the other wheel too.

An inclined plane is higher at one end. This makes it easier to move things.

A pulley is made up of a wheel and a rope. It can lift, lower, or move an object sideways.

Simple Machines

This axe is a wedge.

Machines are tools. They help us do work. A **simple machine** has few or no moving parts.

A wedge is a simple machine that pushes things apart. A lever is used to move things. Screws are simple machines that hold things together.

A screwdriver can be used as a lever.

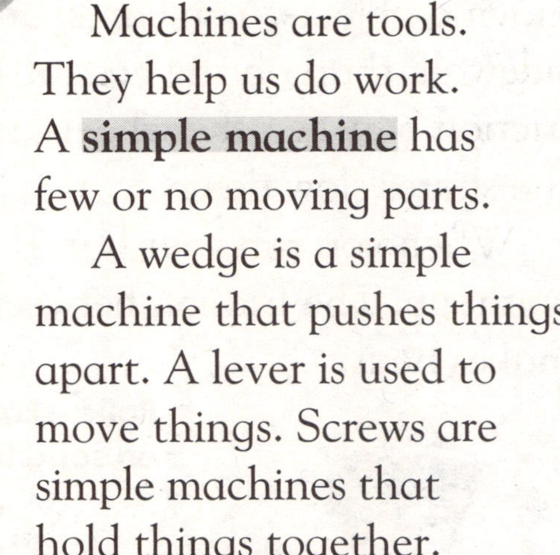

A screw is a simple machine.

When you push a shopping cart, you are doing work. It takes more work to push a heavy cart than to pick up a pencil. That is because you use more force to move the cart.

It takes a lot of work to move a heavy shopping cart.

A gentle kick uses little force.   A hard kick uses great force.

Changing the Way Things Move

You use more force the farther you move an object. An object will not move very far if you push it gently. If you push it hard, it will go far.

You are doing work when you push a light object across the floor. You would do more work if you pushed a heavy object across the floor.

Friction

Friction is a force. It slows down or stops moving objects. You can skate faster on the sidewalk than on the beach. That is because friction between the wheels and the sand makes the skates slow down.

When you rub your hands together, they warm up. The friction between your hands makes heat.

Roller-skating on sand is hard!

Roller-skating on the sidewalk is easier.

132

All About Sound

by Kirsten Anderson

Genre	Comprehension Skill	Text Features	Science Content
Nonfiction	Important Details	• Glossary • Labels • Captions	Sound

Scott Foresman Science 2.11

PEARSON
Scott Foresman

DK

ISBN 0-328-13800-2

9 780328 138005

90000

scottforesman.com

What did you learn?

1. How can an object make sound?

2. What is the difference between *loudness* and *pitch?*

3. **Writing** in Science Snapping shrimp make sounds like popping a balloon. Write to explain how this works.

4. **Important Details** You can make sound travel through string. Page 19 tells you how to do this. What are the important details you need to know to make this work?

Picture Credits
Every effort has been made to secure permission and provide appropriate credit for photographic material.
The publisher deeply regrets any omission and pledges to correct errors called to its attention in subsequent editions.

Photo locators denoted as follows: Top (T), Center (C), Bottom (B), Left (L), Right (R), Background (Bkgd).

2 Aflo Photo/Alamy Images; 9 (CL) ©Jerry Young/DK Images; 14 Chad Slattery/Getty Images; 16 Doug Perrine/Nature Picture Library; 22 (TR) Fred Bavendam/Minden Pictures; 23 Alan Curtis/Alamy Images.

Scott Foresman/Dorling Kindersley would also like to thank: 7 (TL), 9 (TR) Stephen Oliver/DK Images; 20 (C) Natural History Museum, London/DK Images.

ISBN: 0-328-13800-2

Glossary

loudness	how loud or quiet a sound is
pitch	how low or high a sound is
vibrate	to move quickly back and forth

All About Sound

by Kirsten Anderson

What is sound?

Stop and listen. What do you hear?
Maybe you hear voices. Maybe you
hear cars. Maybe you hear birds singing.
You might even hear music playing.

Sound Is All Around You

Now you know how sound is made. Sound
can be loud or soft. Sound can be high pitched
or low pitched. Sound can travel fast or slow.
Next time you are outside, listen to the sounds
around you. The world is full of sound!

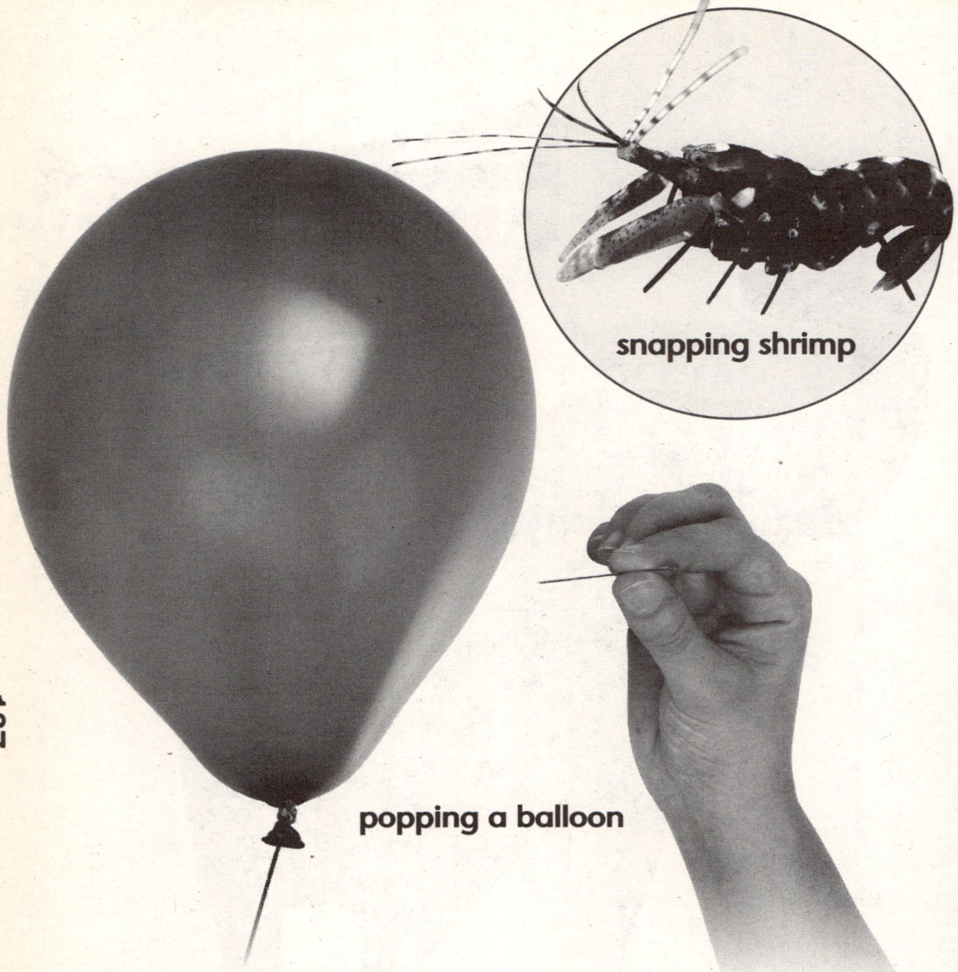

snapping shrimp

popping a balloon

Snapping shrimp make sounds with their large claws. The shrimp open and close their claws fast. They catch air bubbles in their claws. Then the bubbles pop. This works like popping a balloon.

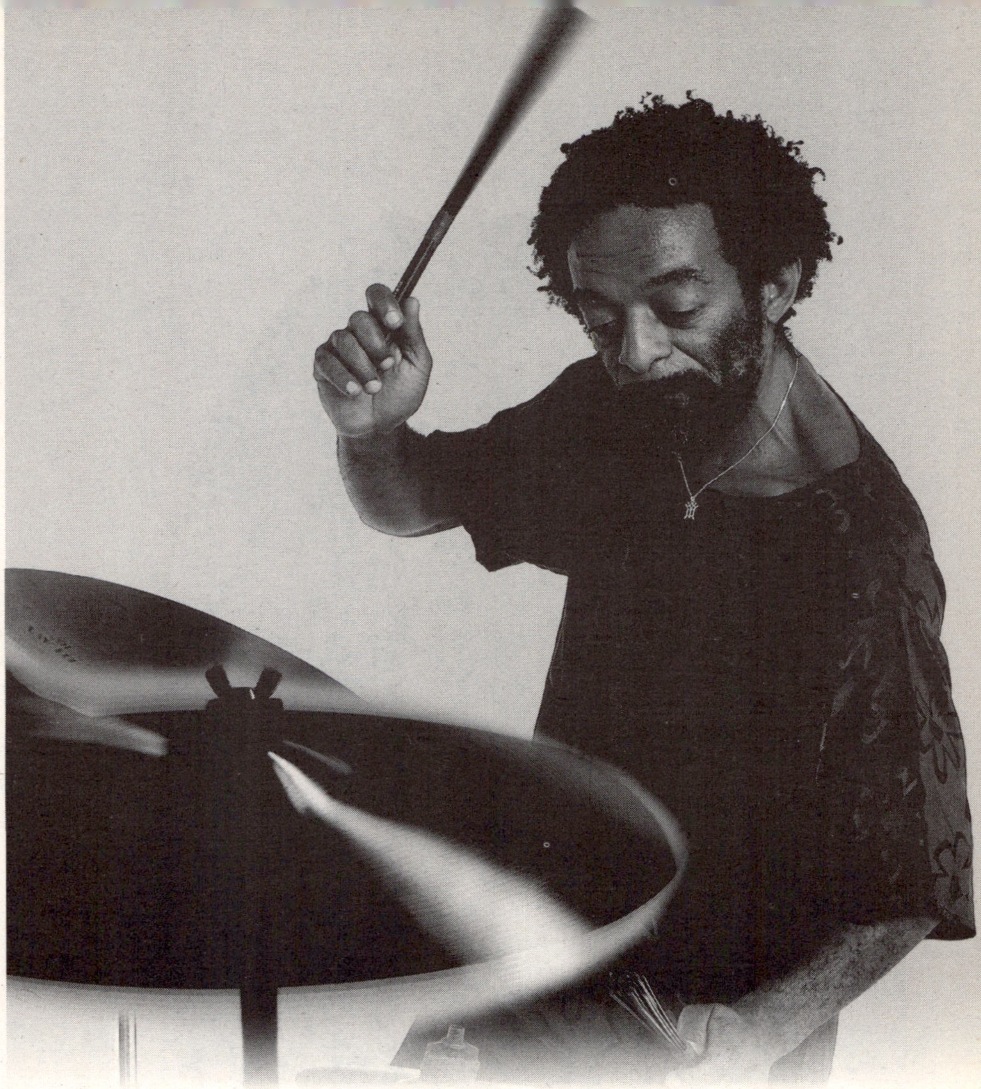

Those are all different sounds. Sound is made when an object vibrates. **Vibrate** means to move quickly back and forth.

When you sing, parts of your throat vibrate.
Put your fingers on the front of your throat
and talk. Do you feel the buzz under your fingers?
Those are your vocal cords vibrating.

Elephants blow air through their trunks.
Their trunks vibrate. This works like playing
a bugle.

Animal Sounds

Animals make sounds using parts of their bodies. Cicadas vibrate small parts of their bellies. This works like tiny drums.

A guitar has strings. When the strings vibrate, they make sound. You can see the guitar strings in this picture.

Loudness

Sounds are not all the same. They are different in some ways. **Loudness** is one way to explain different sounds. Sound can be loud or soft.

Take two cups. Tie them together with a long piece of string. Stand in one room with one cup. Send a friend to another room with the other cup. Pull the string tight. Speak into the cup. Your friend will quickly hear your voice.

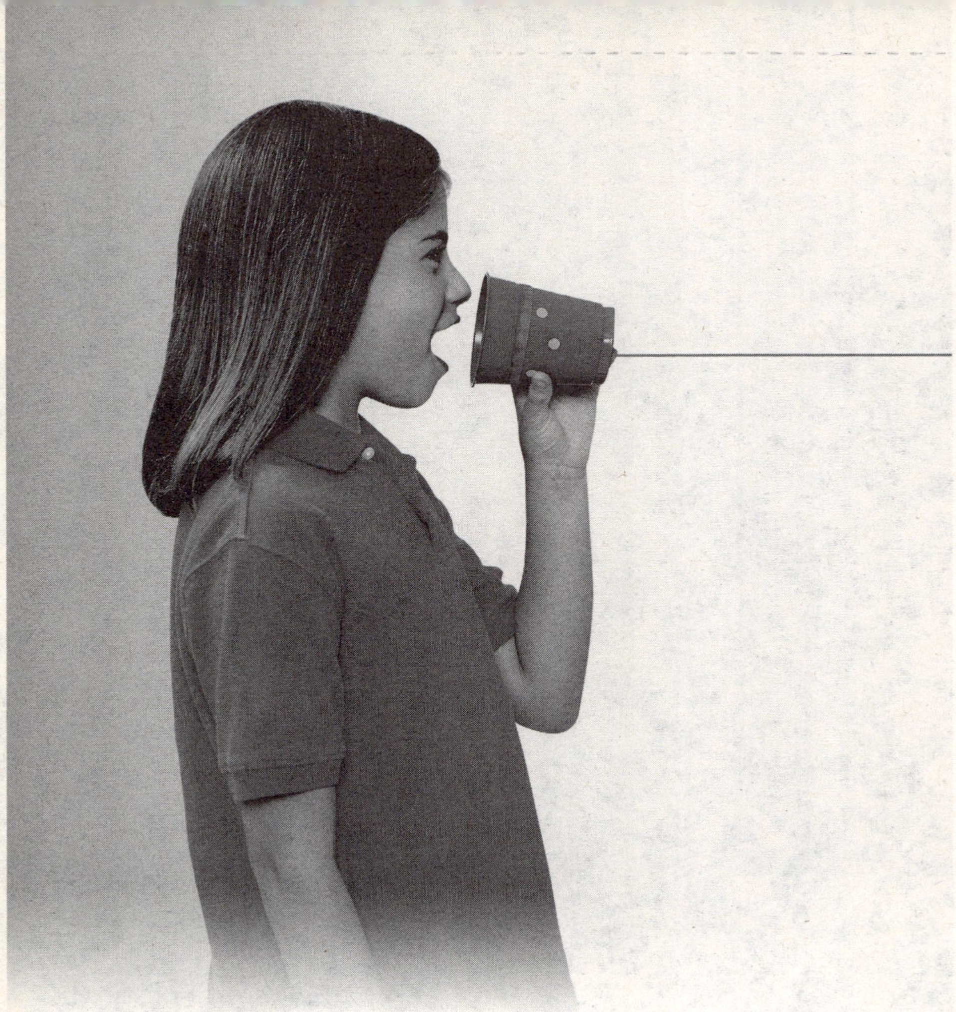

Sound travels through solids. Sound travels faster through solids than through either gases or liquids.

A string is a solid. Sound can travel through string.

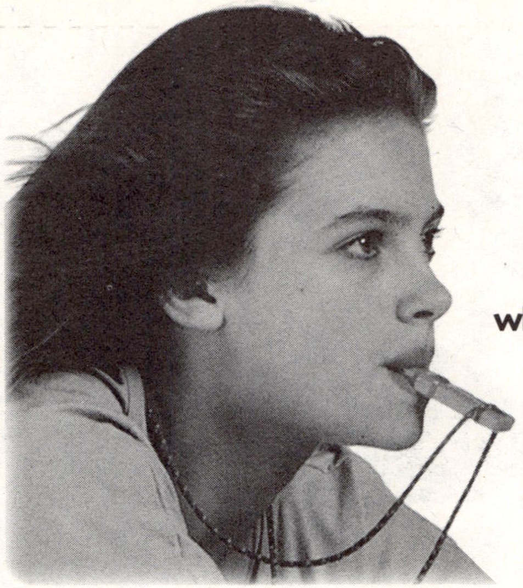

whistle

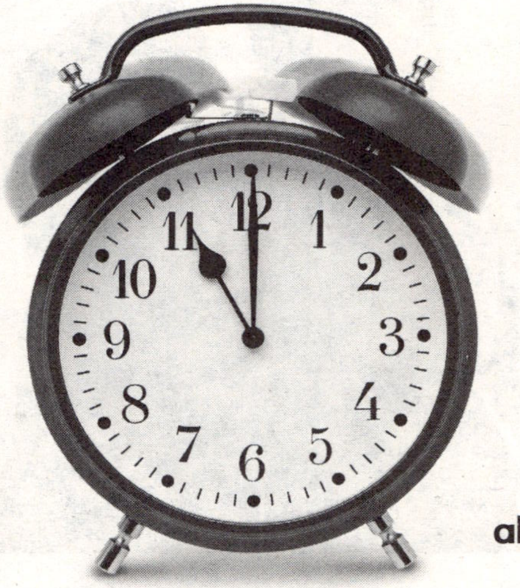

alarm clock

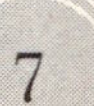

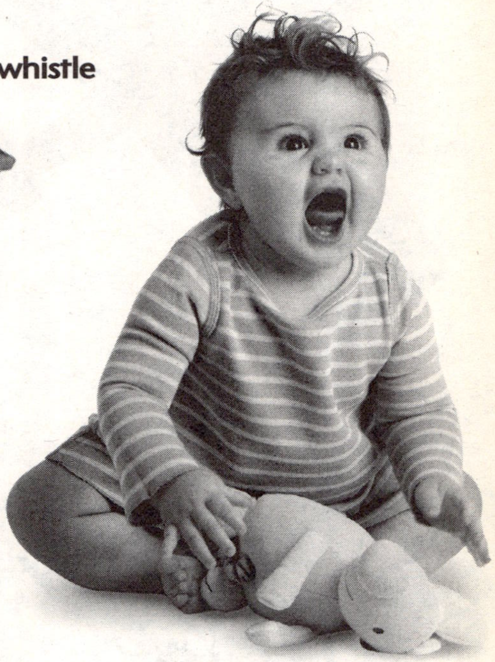

baby

Sound can be loud. Look at the pictures. These things make loud sounds. You can make a loud sound when you shout.

paper airplane

butterfly

whispering

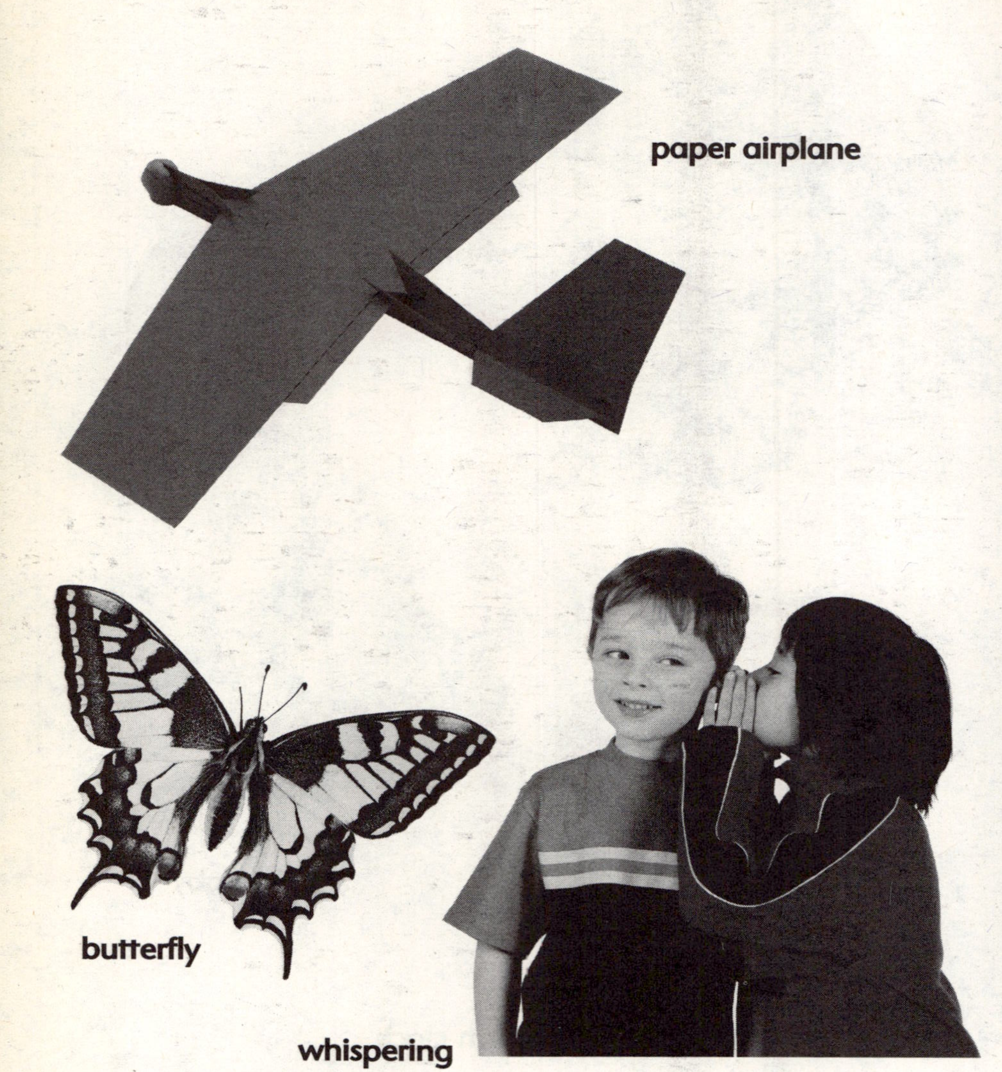

Sound can be soft. The things in these pictures make soft sounds. You can make a soft sound when you whisper.

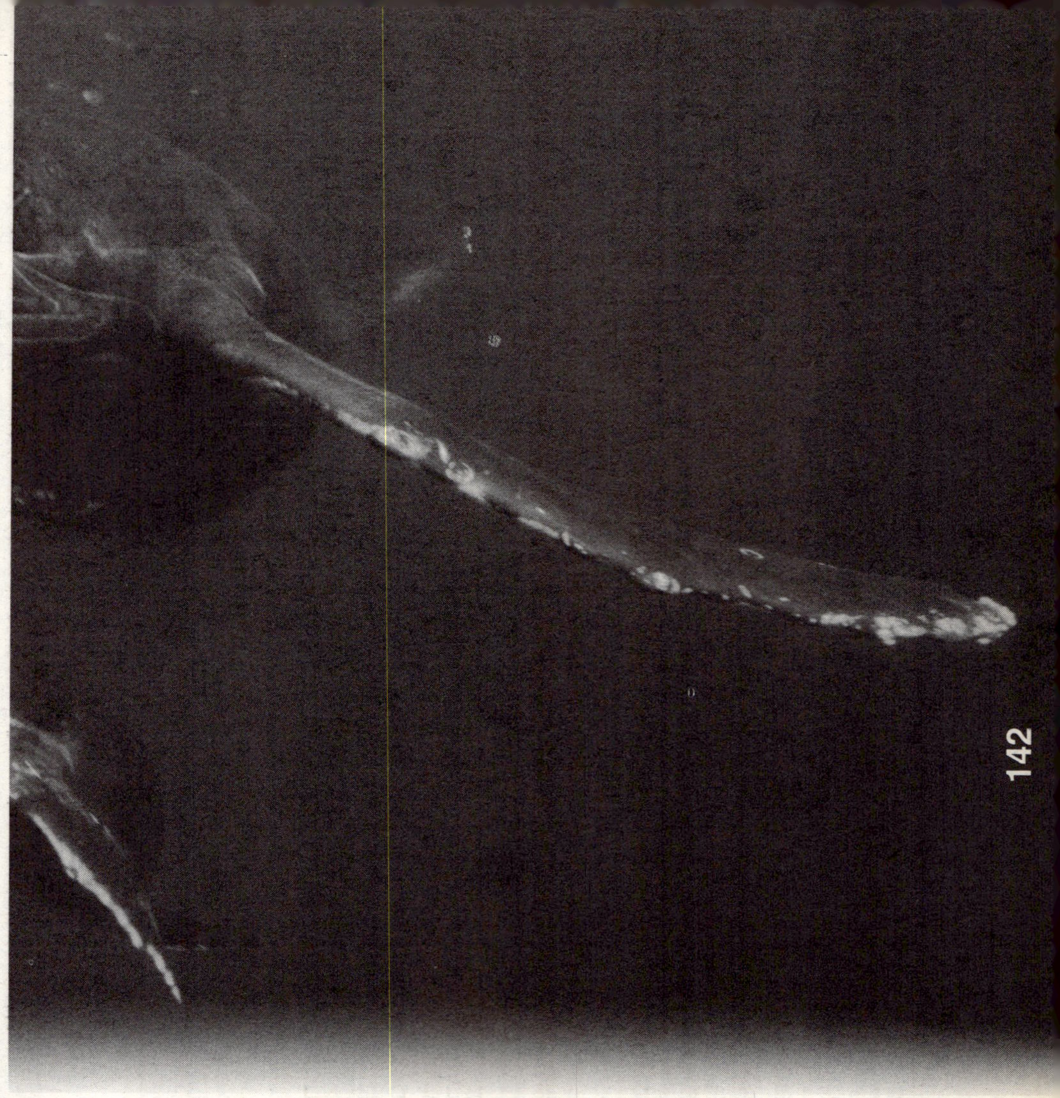

Whales make sounds. Their sounds travel through water. Other whales can hear these sounds many miles away.

Water is a liquid. Sound can travel through liquids. Sound travels faster through liquids than through gases. Sound travels faster through water than through air.

Pitch

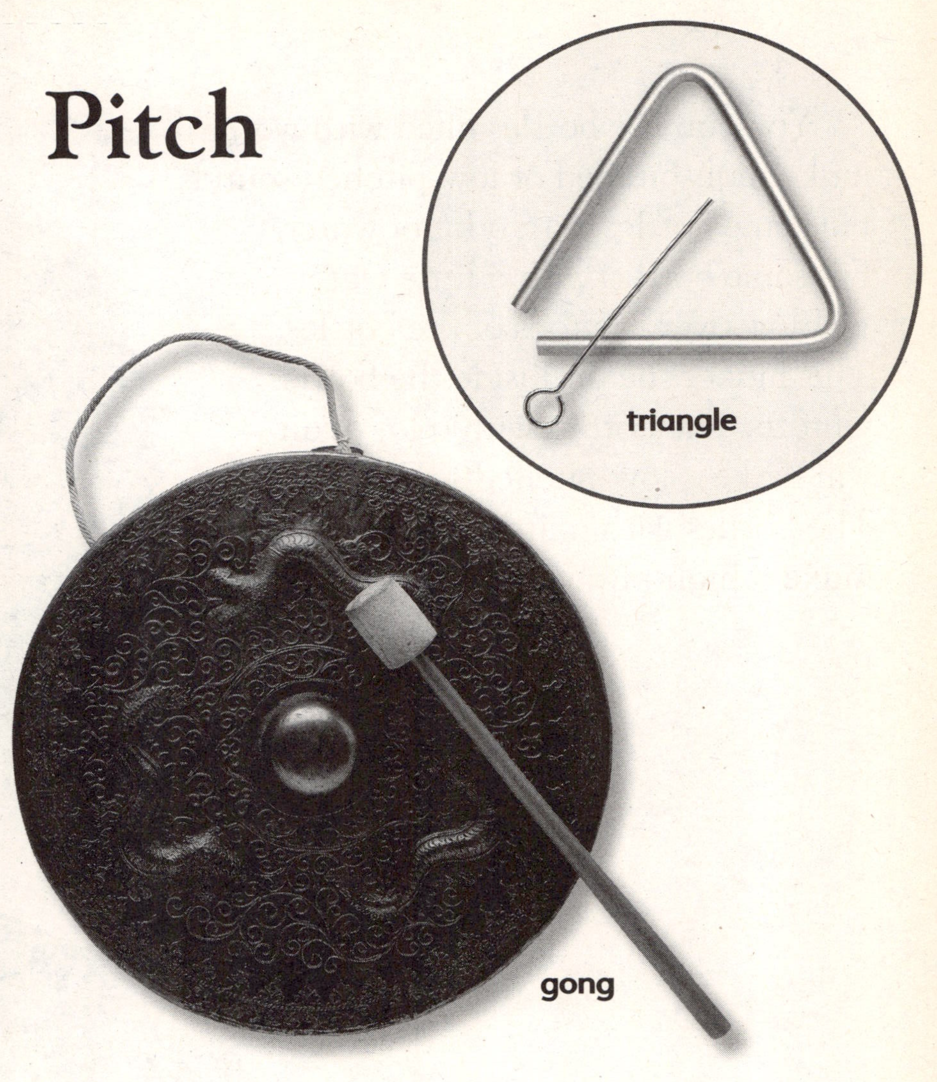

Pitch is another way to explain sound. Pitch can be high or low. Objects that vibrate quickly make a high-pitched sound. Objects that vibrate slowly make a low-pitched sound.

You can use bottles filled with water to
make high-pitched or low-pitched sounds.
Fill some bottles with a lot of water.
Fill some bottles with a little water.

Blow over the tops of the bottles.
This makes the air inside the bottles
vibrate. The bottles with a lot of air
will make a low-pitched sound.
The bottles with a little air will
make a high-pitched sound.

Blow over the tops of bottles of water. The bottles will make different sounds.

Look at the picture of the roller coaster.
The riders are shouting.

The other people in the park can hear them.
They can hear them because sound travels
through air.

Sound Travels

Sound can move through gases, liquids, and solids.

Sound travels through gases. Air is a gas.

Animals make sounds with different pitches.
A lion's roar has a low pitch. A cat's meow
has a high pitch.

Look at the pictures. Which ones show
high-pitched sounds? Which ones show
low-pitched sounds?

146

Science

Science

Space and Technology

Exploring Earth and Space

by Wolf Shelton

Genre	Comprehension Skill	Text Features	Science Content
Nonfiction	Alike and Different	• Captions • Labels • Diagrams • Glossary	Earth and Space

Scott Foresman Science 2.12

PEARSON

Scott Foresman

DK

scottforesman.com

ISBN 0-328-13803-7

90000

9 780328 138036

What did you learn?

1. Why is the Sun important for living things?

2. What is a crater?

3. **Writing** in Science The solar system is everything that moves, or orbits, around our Sun. On your own paper, write to tell about some of the planets, or other objects in our solar system. Use words from the book as you write.

4. Alike and Different How are the Sun and the Moon alike? How are they different?

Picture Credits
Every effort has been made to secure permission and provide appropriate credit for photographic material.
The publisher deeply regrets any omission and pledges to correct errors called to its attention in subsequent editions.

Photo locators denoted as follows: Top (T), Center (C), Bottom (B), Left (L), Right (R), Background (Bkgd).

Opener: Planetary Visions Ltd/Photo Researchers, Inc.; 1 Getty Images; 3 Getty Images; 4 (TR) Getty Images; 5 (Bkgd) Brand X Pictures, (B) image100; 9 ©Comstock Inc.; 10 Brand X Pictures; 14 ©Roger Ressmeyer/Corbis; 15 ©Roger Ressmeyer/Corbis; 16 (T) Mike Segar/Reuters/Corbis, (BR) Getty Images; 19 (TR) Mike Segar/Reuters/Corbis; 20 NASA Image Exchange; 23 (CR) ©JPL/NASA.

Scott Foresman/Dorling Kindersley would also like to thank: 17 NASA/DK Images; 19 (CA) NASA/DK Images; 22 (TR, CRB, CLA) NASA/DK Images, (CLB) NASA/Finley Holiday Films/DK Images; 23 (C) Jet Propulsion Lab (JPL)/DK Images.

Unless otherwise acknowledged, all photographs are the copyright © of Dorling Kindersley, a division of Pearson.

ISBN: 0-328-13803-7

Exploring Earth and Space

by Wolf Shelton

Glossary

axis	an imaginary line through the center of Earth
constellation	a group of stars that form a picture
crater	a bowl-shaped hole on a moon or planet made by crashing rocks
orbit	a path around something
phase	the Moon's shape that we can see
rotation	movement around an axis
solar system	the nine planets and other objects that orbit around the Sun

149

24

The Sun

Stars are made of hot, glowing gases. The Sun is a star. It is made of hot, glowing gases.

The Sun is the closest star to Earth. This is why it looks bigger and brighter than other stars. The Sun is so big and bright that you cannot see other stars during the day.

Look at the picture of our solar system. Can you find the Sun in the middle? Can you name the other planets?

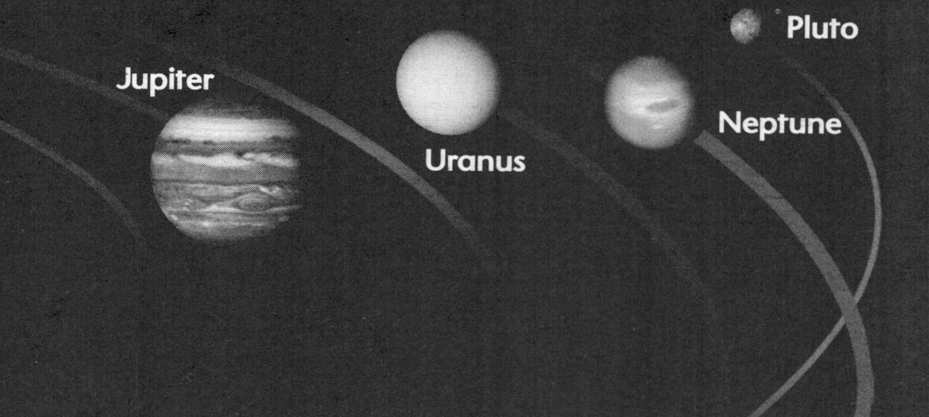

The Solar System

The solar system is everything that moves, or orbits, around the Sun. This includes the nine planets and their moons. Earth is one of the nine planets.

This is a photo of the Sun in space.

We Need the Sun

The Sun is much larger than Earth. It looks small in the sky because it is very far away. One million Earths could fit inside the Sun!

Sometimes you cannot see the Moon at all. This is because none of the Sun's light is touching the Moon.

The shape of the light part of the Moon is called a **phase**.

Sometimes the Moon looks like a circle. You
are looking at one lit up side of the Moon.
Sometimes the Sun only shines on a little part
of the Moon.

The Sun is important for life on Earth.
The Sun gives heat and light. People, plants,
and animals need heat and light to live.

Day and Night

This picture shows a line through the center of Earth. The line is not real. It is imaginary. It is called Earth's axis.

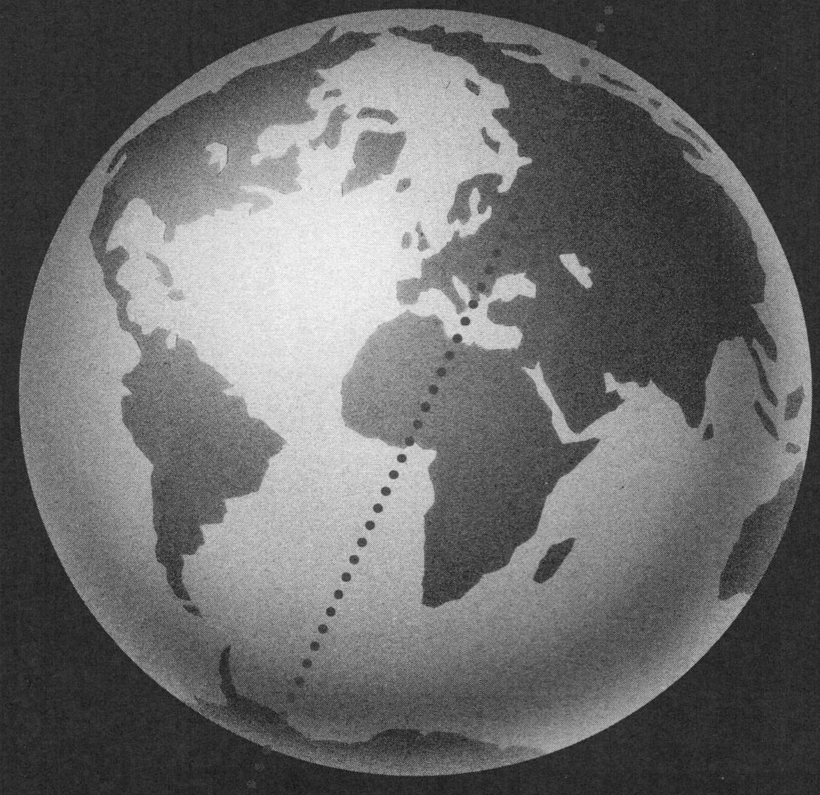

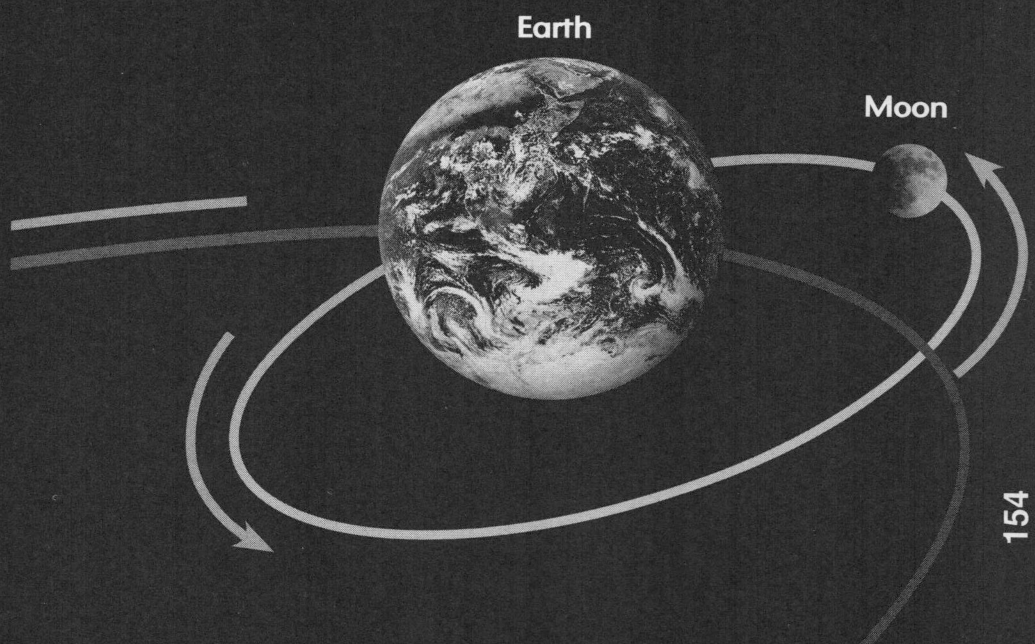

The Moon looks like it changes shape each night. Really, the Moon always stays the same shape. When you see the Moon from Earth you are seeing light from the Sun falling on the Moon in different ways.

The Moon's Changes

Earth moves in an orbit around the Sun. At the same time, the Moon moves in an orbit around Earth. It takes about four weeks for the Moon to make one orbit around Earth.

Can you trace Earth's orbit and the Moon's orbit with your finger?

Earth is always moving in a circle around its axis. Moving around an axis is called **rotation**. Each day Earth makes one rotation.

Earth rotates, or moves, around its axis.

Day and night happen because Earth rotates.

For some hours, the part of Earth where you live faces the Sun. Then it is daytime for you. For some hours, the part of Earth where you live faces away from the Sun. Then it is nighttime for you.

The Moon has deep craters. A crater is a big hole. Large rocks from space crashed into the Moon and made craters. The Moon also has mountains.

156

Why does the Sun move in the sky?

The Sun looks like it moves in the sky. It does not really move. Earth turns on its axis and moves in and out of the Sun's light. This makes it seem like the Sun is moving across the sky.

The Moon

The Moon is the brightest object we can see in the night sky. Sometimes you can see the Moon in the daytime.

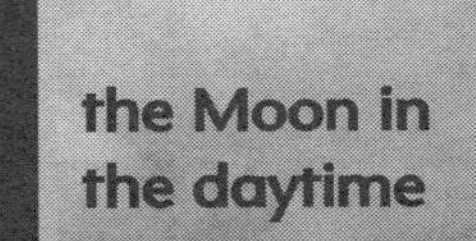

the Moon in the daytime

In the morning when the Sun rises, it is low
in the sky. We talk about the Sun coming up,
but really, the part of Earth where you live is just
moving into the Sun's light.

At noon the Sun looks like it is in the middle
of the sky.

The Sun is a huge star close to Earth.
This is why you can see the Sun in the
daytime. You can see other stars at night.
They look smaller than the Sun because
they are very far away.

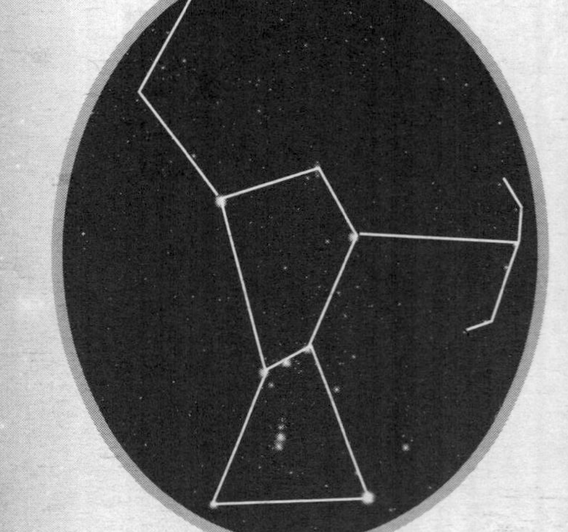

The bright stars in
Orion make the
shape of a hunter.

158

People made up stories about stars. They
imagined lines connecting groups of stars,
like a game of "Connect the Dots." Each
picture they saw is called a **constellation.**
Constellations are groups of stars.

The Night Sky

In the evening, it may look like the Sun is moving down. Really, the part of Earth where you live is moving out of the Sun's light. The Sun does not go away. It shines on the other side of Earth. You just cannot see it where you live.

noon Sun

sunset

You can see the constellation Orion in the sky. Find the three bright stars in a line that make his belt.

Seasons

Earth is tilted on its axis. Earth also moves around the Sun. It takes one year for Earth to move all the way around the Sun. Earth's movement around the Sun is called its **orbit.** Earth's tilt and its orbit around the Sun make seasons happen.

When the part of Earth where you live tilts toward the Sun, it is summer or spring. When the part of Earth where you live tilts away from the Sun, you have winter or fall.

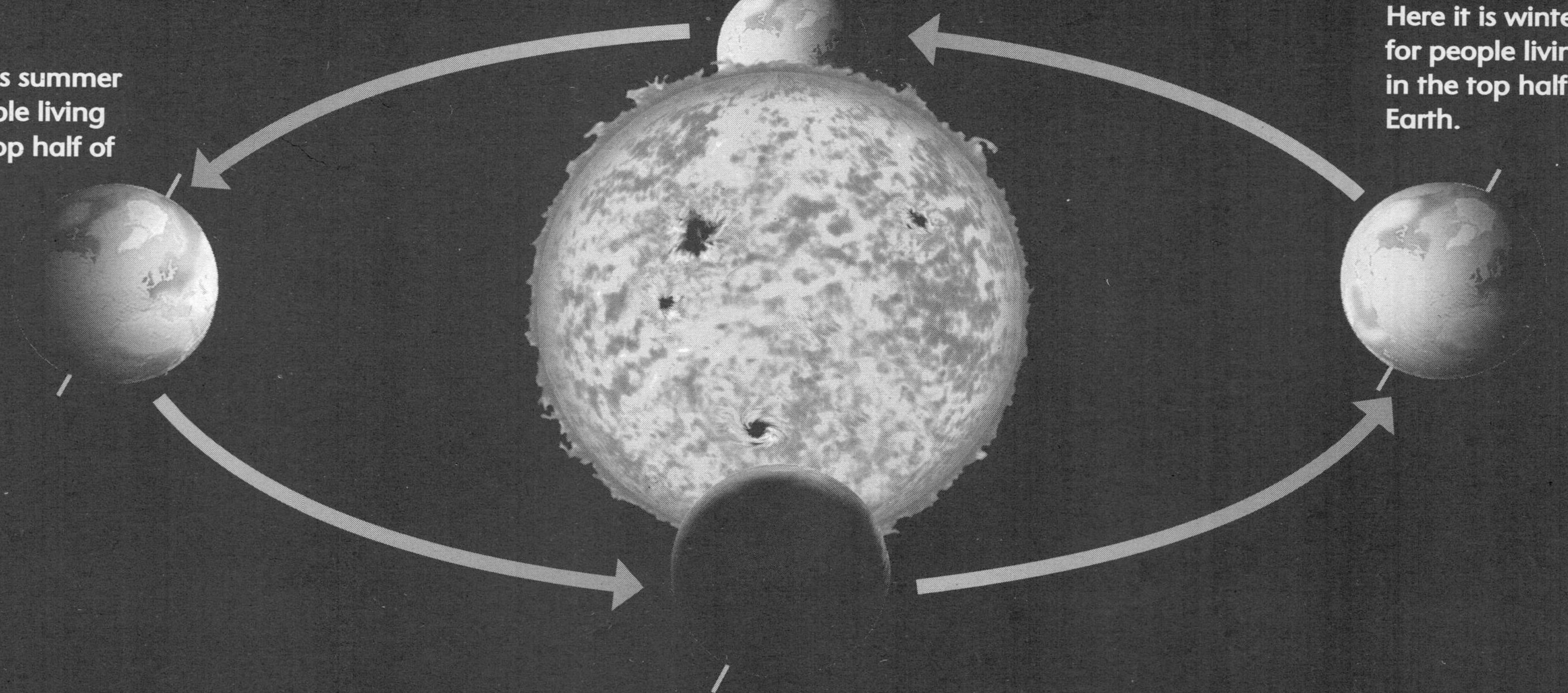

Technology

by Wolf Shelton

Genre	Comprehension Skill	Text Features	Science Content
Nonfiction	Retell	• Call Outs • Captions • Labels • Glossary	Technology

Scott Foresman Science 2.13

PEARSON

Scott Foresman

scottforesman.com

ISBN 0-328-13806-1

9 780328 138067

90000

What did you learn?

1. What are some examples of technology?

2. What is something that is manufactured using machines?

3. **Writing** in Science Technology is all around us. On your own sheet of paper, write about how you use technology.

4. **Retell** Read page 13. In your own words retell how a meteorologist uses technology.

Picture Credits
Every effort has been made to secure permission and provide appropriate credit for photographic material.
The publisher deeply regrets any omission and pledges to correct errors called to its attention in subsequent editions.

Photo locators denoted as follows: Top (T), Center (C), Bottom (B), Left (L), Right (R), Background (Bkgd).

7 (CL) Pallava Bagla/Corbis; 8 Pete Saloutos/Corbis.

Scott Foresman/Dorling Kindersley would also like to thank: 13 NASA/DK Images.

Unless otherwise acknowledged, all photographs are the copyright © of Dorling Kindersley, a division of Pearson.

ISBN: 0-328-13806-1

Glossary

engine	a machine that does work or makes something move
invent	to make something for the first time
manufacture	to make by hand or by machine
meteorologist	a person who studies weather
satellite	an object that revolves around another object
technology	using science to help us solve problems
transportation	the way people or things move from place to place
vaccine	a medicine that can help prevent a disease

Technology

by Wolf Shelton

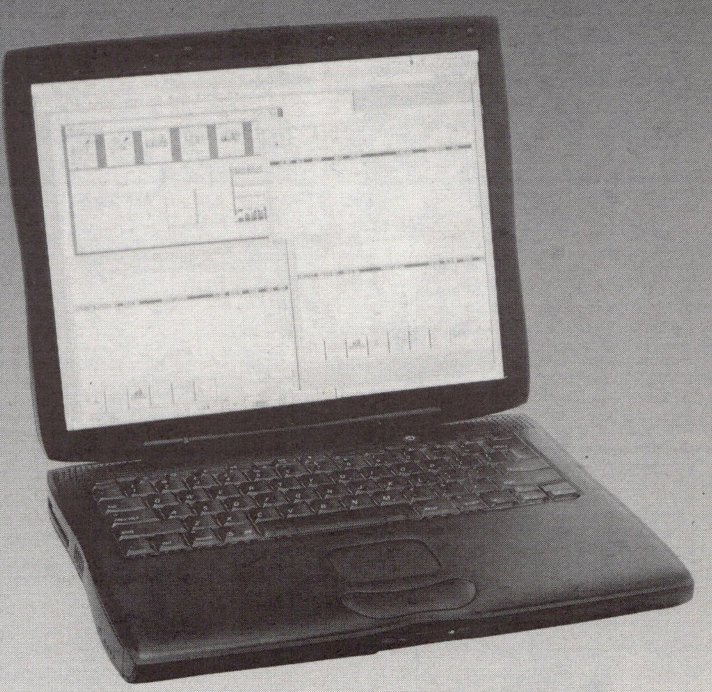

Technology

We can see technology all around us. People drive cars. They use computers. They watch TV. You probably have a refrigerator and a stove in your house. **Technology** means using science to help us solve problems.

Technology is all around us. It has changed the way people live. Pay attention to the tools you use for fun and for work. When do you use technology?

Roller coasters were invented using technology.

Making Things

Manufacture means to make things.
People manufacture things by hand or
by machine. Sometimes the materials used
to manufacture things are found in nature.
Sometimes they are made by people.

The pencils below were manufactured with
the help of machines. They are made from wood.
Wood is found in nature. The erasers are made
of rubber. Most rubber is made by people.

A train is an invention that we use for traveling.

People use technology to invent things. **Invent**
means to make something for the first time.

Inventions can be things we need. Bicycles and
trains are inventions we need to travel. Inventions
can be things we use for fun, such as a skateboard
or a compact disc player.

Transportation

Transportation is the way people or things move from place to place. Technology has changed transportation. It has made transportation faster and safer. The pictures below show one way transportation has changed.

In the past, people used horses for transportation. Today, we use cars, trains, boats, and planes.

Technology helps people do work. A **meteorologist** is a person who studies weather using special machines. A **satellite** is an object that revolves around another object. This satellite sends pictures from space back to Earth. Meteorologists can learn about the weather from these pictures.

satellite

Technology For Fun and Work

People can have fun with technology. Some games use technology. People can watch TV and take photos because of technology.

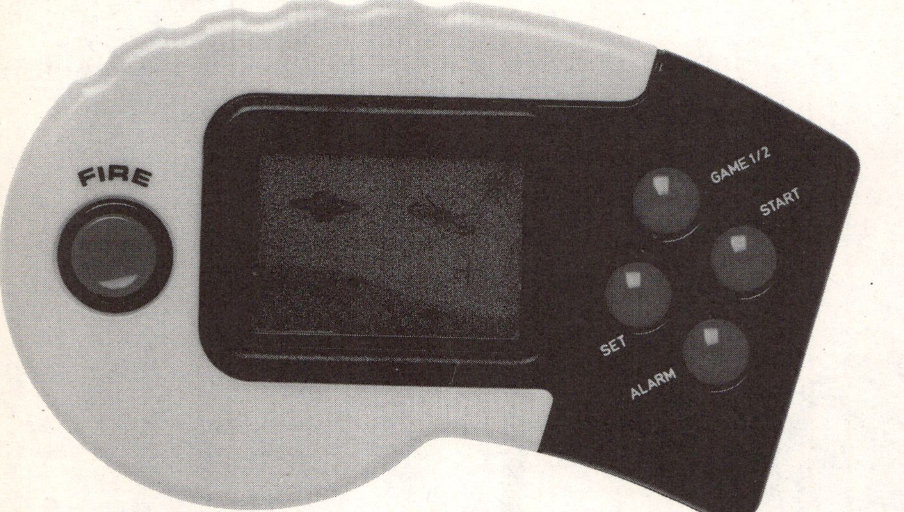

Technology can make fun hand-held video game machines.

Safety and Pollution
Seat belts and air bags have made car travel safer. New cars that make less pollution are being invented.

Many machines have engines. This car has an engine. An **engine** is a machine that does work or makes something move. Early trains used steam engines to move. Today, most machines use gasoline or electricity to move.

Technology can make our lives easier. This vacuum cleaner makes cleaning easier.

Technology Helps Us

Technology has helped people live healthier lives. Vaccines were invented because of technology. A **vaccine** is a medicine that can keep people from getting sick.

Maybe you received a vaccine for a disease called measles.

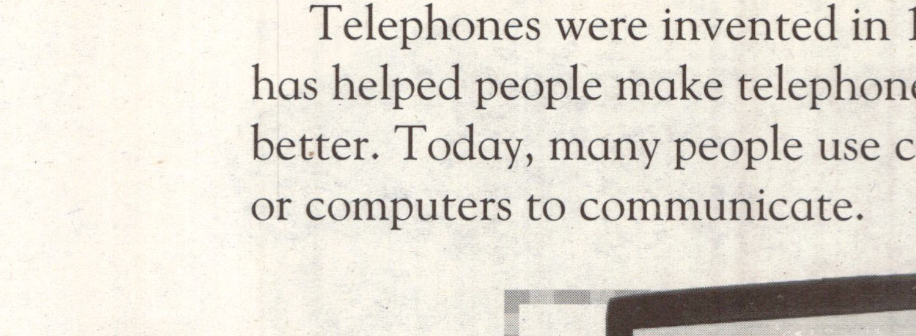

vaccine

Telephones were invented in 1876. Technology has helped people make telephones smaller and better. Today, many people use cell phones or computers to communicate.

Computers were invented in 1946. The first computer filled one whole room! Today's computers are much smaller.

Communication

People communicate, or talk to each other, in many ways. Technology has changed the way people communicate.

People used to communicate only by mail. Technology helped people invent other ways to communicate.

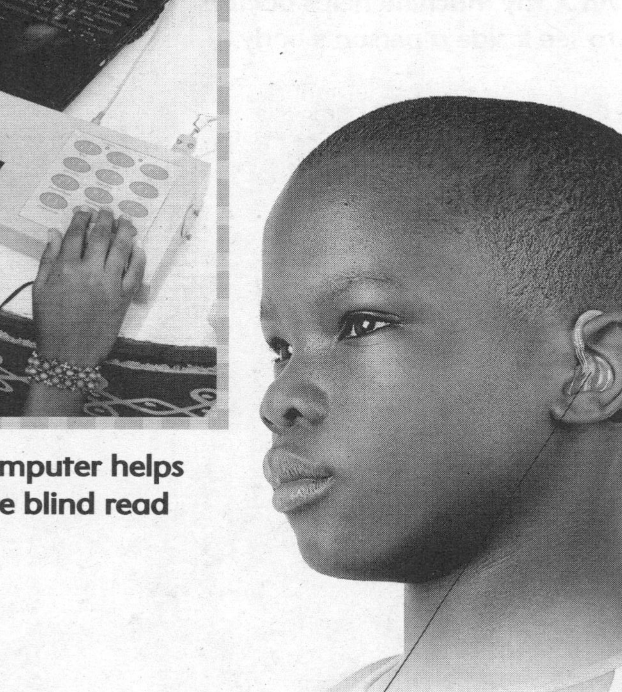

This special computer helps people who are blind read and write.

Doctors use technology to help people hear, see, and walk. A hearing aid is an invention that helps people hear better.

Technology has helped people invent special tools. Doctors use special tools to see inside a person's body. This way they can tell how to help a sick person.

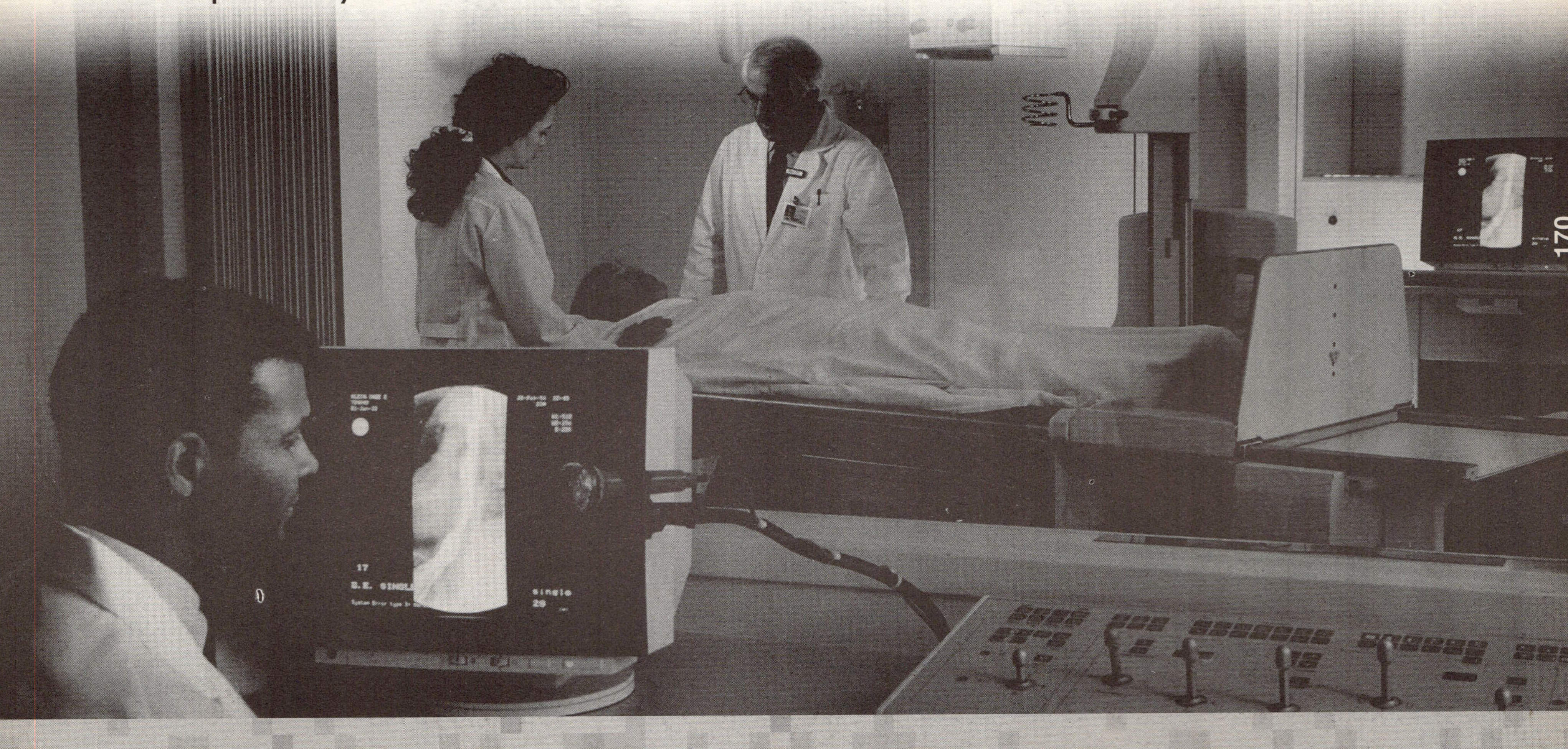

An X-ray machine helps doctors to see inside a person's body.

An X-ray machine is an invention that can take pictures of broken bones. The doctor can see the broken bones even though they are inside the person's body. Then the doctor can make a plan to fix these bones.